T0272235

.

Homeland
of Dreams

Homeland of Dreams

The Epic Journey of a Herd of Asian Elephants in China

By the Writing Group of *Homeland of Dreams*

Books Beyond Boundaries

ROYAL COLLINS

Homeland of Dreams:
The Epic Journey of a Herd of Asian Elephants in China

By the Writing Group of *Homeland of Dreams*

First published in 2022 by Royal Collins Publishing Group Inc.
Groupe Publication Royal Collins Inc.
BKM Royalcollins Publishers Private Limited

Headquarters: 550-555 boul. René-Lévesque O Montréal (Québec) H2Z1B1 Canada
India office: 805 Hemkunt House, 8th Floor, Rajendra Place, New Delhi 110008

Original Edition © Yunnan Education Publishing House Co., Ltd.
This English edition is authorized by Yunnan Education Publishing House Co., Ltd.

ISBN: 978-1-4878-1014-6

To find out more about our publications, please visit www.royalcollins.com.

In Praise of Auspicious Elephants

In colorful Yunnan, where myriad creatures live in harmony, people faithfully protect the splendid vitality created by the spirits of their lives. From spring 2020 to autumn 2021, a group of "auspicious" elephants had a magical tour in the land of wonders. Throughout their journey, many people devoted themselves to the protection of these "elves" from the forest. In uniforms that were the same color as our flourishing planet, they followed the elephants through the luxuriantly green land full of life. It is a land where fish swim freely in clear waters, where peacocks dance elegantly in lush mountains, and where elephants roam peacefully in beautiful communities. It is a country that adores harmonious coexistence between humans and nature, a community of life, and a homeland of dreams for all.

Foreword

"China has made remarkable progress in building an ecological civilization. The recent story of the northward travel and return of a group of elephants in Yunnan Province in southwestern China shows the vivid results of our endeavor to protect wild animals." On the afternoon of October 12, 2021, President Xi Jinping attended the leaders' summit of the 15th meeting of the Conference of the Parties to the Convention on Biological Diversity held in Kunming via video link and delivered a keynote speech. In it, he specifically mentioned the wild Asian elephant in Yunnan and said: "China will continue to advance ecological progress, stay committed to implementing the new development philosophy emphasizing innovative, coordinated, green and open development for all, and build a beautiful China."

From the spring of 2020 to the autumn of 2021, the wild Asian elephant herd Short Trunks in Yunnan had a magical journey that attracted the attention of the whole world. Cared and protected by people, they crossed mountains and waters over thousands of kilometers across most of the Yunnan Province. The Associated Press and other international media all reported on "China's wandering elephants becoming international stars."

The Chinese say "peace has an image," which comes in the shape of an "auspicious elephant" in a peaceful world where people live in prosperity and contentment. The story of the Short Trunks shows the world a harmonious, secure, and beautiful China. It reflects the local practice of President Xi's ecological civilization theory and the people's awareness of respecting, accommodating, protecting, and living in harmony with nature.

Over the years, especially since the 18th National Congress of the Communist Party of China (CPC), the Party Central Committee with Comrade Xi Jinping at its core has placed the construction of ecological civilization in a prominent position in the Party's overall work and carried out a series of fundamental, pioneering, and long-term work. The ecological construction project has thus undergone historical and overall changes in both recognition and practice.

With the wild Asian elephants, we smelled the fresh air and saw green trees and clear waters along the way. For more than a year, all parties worked hard to protect the elephants and ensure the safety of the residents where the elephants went. The monitoring personnel stayed with the elephants day and night. They kept the unmanned aerial vehicles (UAVs) above one hundred meters to minimize the disturbance of the herd. The villagers spontaneously prepared corns and pineapples to feed the elephants and welcome their arrival ...

These pictures and details fully delineate the image of a gentle and wildlife-caring country where "all beings flourish when they live in harmony and receive nourishment from nature." Gratifying changes are taking place in China's ecological environment, and the Chinese people's awareness and ability in ecological protection are also increasing. The eastern superpower is taking up its responsibility in building a shared future for all life on Earth.

All approach the one who holds the *Dao*. Being the best example of harmonious coexistence between humans and nature, the round trip journey of wild Asian elephants in Yunnan warms the hearts of the world. Foreign media, officials, and the public praised the Chinese government and people's efforts during the Short Trunks' magical journey. Through this journey, an ecological, harmonious, and responsible China was presented to the world in a true, three-dimensional, and comprehensive form.

President Xi said the Yunnan elephants exemplified the ideology "If we humans do not fail nature, nature will not fail us." When they "chased" the elephants, many monitoring staff mentioned that these smart "elves" seemed to have reached an agreement with humans, and they expressed their gratitude in their own way. We also thank them for writing the most touching ecological story in Yunnan.

On the evening of August 8, 2021, the elephants passed the Yuanjiang River Bridge and walked away into the night.

The epic journey of the Short Trunks has come to an end, but the story of humans and wild Asian elephants is not over. It will continue to live in praise into the future. We see a homeland of dreams with abundant vitality, the place where all lives yearn to be. We see a beautiful country in the East, the practitioner of green development, leading the world to an ecological civilization from micro to macro.

"We need to have deep reverence for nature, respect nature, follow nature's laws and protect nature, so as to build a homeland of harmonious coexistence between man and nature." The story of Yunnan's wild Asian elephants is the epitome of the community of life. In a bigger realm, in a longer time frame, and in a dazzling new era, we can do so much more.

Contents

July 15, 2021. The Short Trunks are enjoying the view on the top of the mountain.
Shiyantou Village, Shiping County, Honghe Prefecture.

❖ *June 19, 2021. The Short Trunks.*
   Diesuo Village, Dalongtan Township, Eshan County.

❖ *The Asian elephants living in a national park.*

August 13, 2021. The Short Trunks are wandering in the mountains.
Kunyong Village, Mojiang County, Pu'er City.

June 2021. The baby elephant is resting by its mother.
Xiyang Village, Jinning District, Kunming City.

❖ *Mother and child playing in the water.*

June 10, 2021. The Short Trunks are crossing the stream.
Zhuomu Old Village, Shijie Township, Yimen County.

July 2021. The "rebellious boy" is wandering alone.
Near the Yulin wine factory, Eshan County.

❖ *July 17, 2021. The resting Short Trunks.*

Shiyantou Village, Longwu Township, Shiping County, Honghe Prefecture.

❖ *The Asian elephants in habitat.*

❖ *August 8, 2021. The Short Trunks are walking across the Yuanjiang River Bridge.*

❖ *September 9, 2021. The Short Trunks are hiding from the sun under the trees.*
  Kafang Village, Tongguan Township, Mojiang County, Pu'er City.

A wild Asian elephant in Xishuangbanna National Nature Reserve.

❖ December 2021. The Short Trunks in habitat.

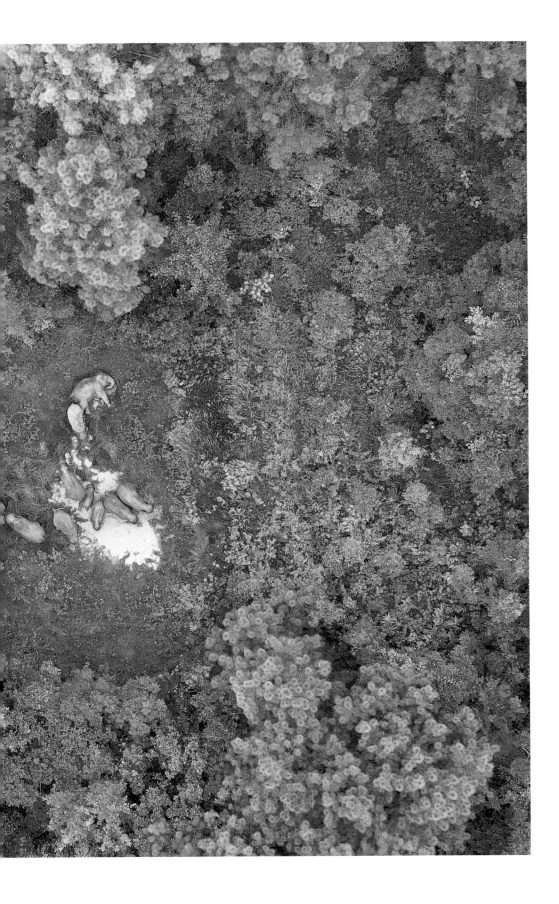

❖ *September 7, 2021. The Short Trunks are eating in the field.*
  Tongguan Township, Mojiang County, Pu'er City.

❖ *June 2021. Clever elephants turn on the tap to have a drink.*
  Shuanghe Yi Township, Jinning District, Kunming City.

❖ *June 9, 2021. An elephant.*
  Zhuomu Old Village, Shijie Township, Yimen County, Yuxi City.

❖ *May 31, 2021. The Short Trunks are crossing the Luo River together.*
Luohe Township, Hongta District, Yuxi City.

❖ *September 4, 2021. Two elephants are enjoying a mud bath.*
Tongguan Township, Mojiang County.

· *The Big Humps.*

❖ *Big Teeth.*

❖ *August 2021. The Short Trunks are walking in the tea plantation. Mojiang County, Pu'er City.*

❖ *Baby Bamboo Teeth.*

An elephant is eating.

❖ *A herd of wild elephants in habitat.*

❖ *July 18, 2021. The Short Trunks are eating and playing in the field.*
  Shiyantou Village Committee, Longwu Township, Shiping County, Honghe Prefecture.

Asian elephants in habitat.

Asian elephants in habitat.

❖ *July 2021. Elephants are playing and eating in a cornfield.*
  Longwu Township, Shiping County, Honghe Prefecture.

❖ *A cute baby elephant is playing in the water.*

July 8, 2021. Elephants are coming.
Nizhe Village, Yangwu Township, Xinping County.

July 15, 2021. The Short Trunks are preparing to rest on Shiyantou Mountain.
Shiyantou Mountain, Longwu Township, Shiping County, Honghe Prefecture.

❖ *The monitoring members of the Yunnan Provincial Forest Fire Brigade become "elephant chasers."*

❖ *The monitoring staff is taking photos of the Shor Trunks from a distance.*

Members in the UAV group are adjusting the drone.

❖ *Monitoring staff at work.*

❖ *August 9, 2021. The Short Trunks are walking together.*
  Crossroad at the Colorful Stone Forest, Yuanjiang County, Yuxi City.

❖ *July 2021. The elephants are passing by the monitoring staff.*
  Shiyantou Village, Longwu Township, Shiping County, Honghe Prefecture.

July 2021. The Short Trunks are resting with some on guard.
Shiyantou Village, Longwu Township, Shiping County, Honghe Prefecture.

June 7, 2021. The Short Trunks are resting in a woodland.
Laijiaxin Village, Xiyang Township, Jinning District, Kunming City.

❖ *Tropical rainforest in Xishuangbanna.*

❖ *The herd is strolling in the river valley.*

❖ *Asian elephants in habitat.*

Helping Ranran cross the river together.

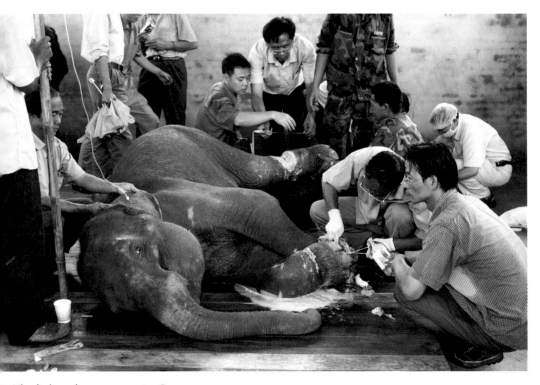

The elephant doctors are treating Ranran.

❖ *The mother elephant is nursing her cub.*

Yunnan Asian Elephant Breeding and Rescue Center.

Many Asian elephants are living peaceful lives in the Wild Elephant Valley.

❖ "Elephant dad" is taking an elephant to field training.

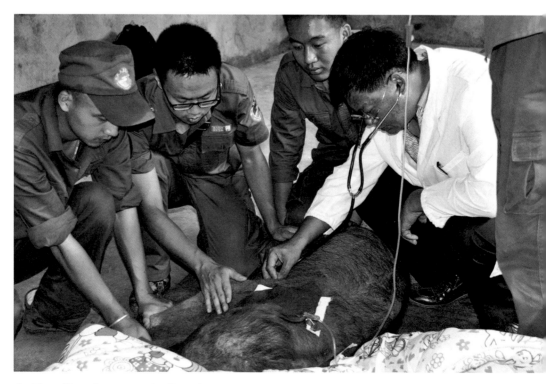

❖ The staff members are treating Yangniu.

• *A staff is taking a walk with the elephants.*

❖ *The staffs are feeding the elephant.*

❖ *An unexpected visitor.*

❖ *The protective fences outside Naji Elementary School.*

❖ *The playground of Naji Elementary School.*

❖ *Xiaopuxi Village.*

❖ *September 9, 2021. The Short Trunks are eating.*
  Kafang Village, Tongguan Township, Mojiang County, Pu'er City.

❖ *July 2021. The Short Trunks are going into the woods.*
Longwu Township, Shiping County, Honghe Prefecture.

❖ *July 17, 2021. The Short Trunks are eating in the field.*
  Near the Shiyantou Village Committee, Longwu Township, Shiping County, Honghe Prefecture.

❖ Humans and elephants live harmoniously together.

❖ An advisor is teaching students about Asian elephants in the rainforest in Xishuangbanna.

❖ *Live broadcast of "Cute Yunnan Broadcast."*

❖ *Activity site of "Cute Yunnan Broadcast."*

❖ *Household damaged by wild elephants.*

❖ *June 12, 2021. The Short Trunks are resting.*
   Nanshan Village, Shijie Township, Yimen County, Yuxi City.

❖ *September 1, 2021. The Short Trunks are heading for the banana plantation.*
   Yangliujing, Mojiang County, Pu'er City.

August 18, 2021. The Short Trunks are walking in the fields.
Dalian Village, Mojiang County, Pu'er City.

❖ *The biodiversity of Yunnan has inspired literary creation.*

❖ *Harmonious coexistence between humans and nature.*

Wu Ran is recommending picture books about elephants.

Fan Yi is working in the field.

❖ *The flower of* Magnolia sinica *captured by Fan Yi.*

❖ *The "Image-driving Defender" award trophy.*

◆ *The* Theloderma bicolor *captured by Fan Yi.*

❖ *September 2, 2021. The Short Trunks are moving.*
Tongguan Township, Mojiang County, Pu'er City.

❖ *The books* Cute Elephants Love Yunnan *and* Travel Notes of Wild Elephants in Yunnan *are officially published.*

❖ *Asian elephants living in tropical rainforest.*

➤ *The elephant sculpture* The Great Wall Ridge of Lives.

❖ *December 2021. The Short Trunks continue to live happily in their habitat.*

❖ *October 9, 2021. The 2021 Erhai Forum on Global Ecological Civilization was held in Dali. More than three hundred Chinese and foreign guests worked together on the road of ecological governance near Erhai Lake.*

The ecological civilization establishment in China allows wildlife to live in a better environment.

* *Asian elephants in habitat.*

❖ *The Wild Elephant Valley Station.*

❖ *Asian elephants in habitat.*

CHAPTER 1

A Peaceful World Has Elephants

"Biodiversity makes Earth full of vigor and vitality, and lays the foundation for human survival and development. Protecting biodiversity helps protect Earth, our common homeland, and contributes to humanity's sustainable development."

—On the afternoon of October 12, 2021, President Xi Jinping attended the leaders' summit of the 15th meeting of the Conference of the Parties to the Convention on Biological Diversity (COP15) held in Kunming via video link and delivered a keynote speech.

Yunnan Province, being only 4.1% of China in geographical space, contains all the types of ecosystems on earth except oceans and deserts. The number of biological species of each major group found in Yunnan accounts for nearly or over half of that of the same species found nationwide, with some located only in this province. It is thus praised as the "kingdom of animals," "kingdom of plants," "world flower garden," and one of the most important treasure houses of biodiversity in the world.

Among all species, the Asian elephant has been enjoying special popularity and protection as one of the flagship species. Chinese people see elephants as auspicious animals because of their calmness and dignity. They are often depicted carrying a treasure bottle on their back, which indicates peace, health, and wealth. Throughout Chinese history, people decorated their homes with bottle-holding elephants made in bronze, jade, porcelain, and other materials to pray for peace and good luck.

However, these beloved animals can be troublesome at times …

In March 2020, the wild Asian elephant family Short Trunks set off from the Mengyang Sub-Reserve in Xishuangbanna National Nature Reserve in Yunnan Province and moved north into the city of Pu'er in July. On April 16, 2021, the elephants entered Yuanjiang County in Yuxi from Mojiang County in Pu'er. They left their traditional habitat and continued to travel north, which attracted worldwide attention.

The herd detoured for thousands of kilometers through the cities of Xishuangbanna, Pu'er, Yuxi, Honghe, and Kunming. In August 2021, after safely crossing the mainstream of the Yuanjiang River, the fourteen Asian elephants moved southward until finally returning to their habitat. Including the adolescent male elephant that had been sent back to Xishuangbanna Nature Reserve earlier, all fifteen wild Asian elephants that migrated north were safely back home. The herd was in an overall good situation, and there was no one hurt either in the human community or in the elephant family along the way.

1

Zoom Out from the Elephants to the Beautiful Big Picture of Biodiversity

The round trip of the wild Asian elephants in Yunnan has made internet "hot searches" nearly twenty times.

The important nodes on their ways, their cute pictures, the reasons for their leaving home, their real-time locations, how can human-elephant conflicts be avoided and other topics have attracted global attention and heated discussions.

Although the Short Trunks only traveled inside of Yunnan, they have made themselves known in many more places and became great ambassadors by telling a wonderful Chinese story to the world.

The Washington Post noticed the herd as early as when it had roamed for 480 kilometers and believed that this was solid proof of an elephant protection achievement. The *Post* told its readers that after twenty years of protection, the number of wild elephants in Xishuangbanna and two adjacent areas has almost doubled to about three hundred. Reuters forwarded the elephants' sleeping positions that went viral on the Internet. The Associated Press also commented: "China's wandering elephants are becoming international stars."

The overseas media that paid the most attention to the Short Trunks was the BBC. It published many relevant reports and quoted the ridicule of Chinese netizens saying that "the elephants were going to attend COP15 in Kunming," in addition to giving a formal introduction to this event. Another British newspaper,

The Guardian, reported that Yunnan had been trying to help the elephants return to their habitat and make them safer.

Japanese media such as TV Asahi, Fuji TV, and TBS TV directly sent out their journalists in China to follow up on the story. While reporting the journey of the Short Trunks, they also enthusiastically introduced to the audience China's geographical features, commenting that only in such a healthy environment could elephants travel safely. In one popular program, the TV Asahi spent nearly thirty minutes making a special report on the northward movement of Asian elephants in Yunnan, which made a considerable viewing rate.

The Times of India reported on the mobilization of thousands of personnel in Yunnan to track the elephants with drones and infrared cameras. Cambodian website Khmerload wrote: "In Yunnan, a group of elephants is moving hundreds of kilometers north. They lie down to rest whenever they feel like doing so, and no one bothers them. It's really harmonious ..."

The elephants have won the praise of major international media. The beautiful sceneries they passed through and the protection measures taken by local governments and people in China also impressed the world.

The Associated Press reported "In China, wild elephants are protected at the highest level, and their status is no less than that of giant pandas." *The Washington Post* also described in detail how elephants and local residents lived in harmony. The Japanese media and animal protection experts were amazed by the "elephant protection lineup," which included manpower, unmanned aerial vehicles (UAV or drones), and vehicles. Some foreign netizens admiringly said: "Elephants know that China is a good country!"

Comments from domestic netizens: "In the face of adorable elephants, even western media could not find anything to judge."

The wonderful journey of the Short Trunks has not only told the world a wonderful story but also helped us find the center of building a shared future for all life on Earth.

Taking the elephant as the "center," we see the tireless and meticulous efforts of the Chinese government and people, we see the ecological value and environmental protection significance of the story, and we see the importance and necessity of building a shared future for all life on Earth.

Now, let's review the wonderful journey of the Short Trunks, to zoom out from the elephants to see the beautiful big picture of the ecosystem and biodiversity painted by the Chinese people.

A Poem from an English Friend to the Elephants

When the Elephants Came to Kunming

When the elephants came to Kunming
The shopkeeper said, "Do come in."
They were rather unsure,
(Hadn't been there before)
Then the rest of the herd followed in.

It soon became clear
There was nothing to fear.
So the elephants then became bold.
There were boxes of shoes
With so many to choose
It was really a sight to behold.

Then with elephant fun
And their shopping done
They left all the chaos behind.

The shopkeeper said, as he fell into bed,
"What a mess—What a sale—Never mind."

Some things were not quite right,
Some shoes were too tight,
But they "Clackety Clicked" on their way.
"Some heels are too high."
They said with a sigh
But "Oh what a wonderful day!"

—**Janet S. Norfolk**

2

The Magic Journey of the Short Trunks

Many years later, we will still enjoy talking about the spring when the elephants set foot on their journey north.

In March 2020, the wild Asian elephant family Short Trunks set off from Mengyang Sub-Reserve in Yunnan Xishuangbanna National Nature Reserve.

They went all the way north over green mountains and clear waters for more than 1,300 kilometers and across five prefectures (cities). They even reached the city of Kunming, the capital of Yunnan Province. At that time, COP15 was about to begin there. That's why people who tracked and followed the elephants joked that they were going to attend the meeting.

Of course, the Short Trunks did not really enter the venue, but they were seen on a much bigger stage.

The theme of COP15 was "Ecological Civilization: Building a Shared Future for All Life on Earth." The harmonious coexistence of people and elephants in Yunnan reflected through the Short Trunks' journey was definitely a good start on this path.

As the old saying goes, "peace has an image." It is now safe to say that elephants are part of that image. Only when the concept of harmonious coexistence between man and nature is profoundly understood and put into action, and when the ecological environment is harmonious and beautiful, can elephants dare to come out for a walk.

Why Are They Called the Short Trunks?

Today, the Short Trunks are well known in the world. This, of course, was most delightful for the monitoring staff who gave them the name.

Elephants mainly live in herds except for adult male individuals. All the wild Asian elephant herds have names. According to the members of the Asian elephant observation and protection group, the names are more like nicknames, which come from features such as ears, front teeth, back, tail and so on, such as Big Teeth, Baby Bamboo Teeth, the Ranran family, the Big Hump family, and the Nicked Ear family, etc.

The name for the Short Trunk family came from the monitoring staff at the Asian elephant monitoring and protection group. During a routine inspection, they found that a female elephant in this family had a shorter trunk than others with no nasal process, so they named the herd the Short Trunks.

Chinese folk people believe that a newborn with a "cheap name" lives a long and healthy life. Short Trunks is not an elegant name, but it is very characteristic. The monitoring members never expected that the elephant with a slightly shorter trunk and her family members would become a global sensation in the future.

Two New Members Are Welcomed on Route

The Short Trunks left their original habitat and had great fun on their way up north. Everyone loves this story, but the birth of new members to the family is definitely the favorite part of all.

Two baby elephants were born during the journey. Being one of the animals with the longest pregnancy in the world, it is not easy for elephants to give birth to a new life. Moreover, the Asian elephants are also listed as Appendix I species in the Convention on International Trade in Endangered Species of Wild Fauna and

Flora (CITES) and are a first-class protected species in China. At present, there are only about 300 wild Asian elephants in China.

Therefore, the arrival of new lives to the Short Trunk family was most exciting to all professional and ordinary "elephant trackers."

Two Asian elephant monitors named Bi Shixue and Fu Qiyou of the Minle Village Committee of Ning'er County, Pu'er City, witnessed a baby elephant soon after it was born. "The baby elephant was protected by the mother under her belly all the time, and we could only steal a peek once in a while. We had to see that the baby elephant was well and healthy every day." They had even thought of a name for the baby. "We don't know if it's male or female. We will call it Gaogao (tall) if it's a boy and Lili (beautiful) if it's a girl because it was born in Gaolizhong."

Becoming "Huge Stars" after a Nap

What made the Short Trunks really famous at home and abroad was the photo of them sleeping.

This picture of the elephants' sleeping position quickly became popular as it gave a glimpse into the daily life of the happy family. The members surround the babies from all sides to protect them—literally in the shape of a heart—even when they are sleeping. It shows that all parents share the same affection and tenderness for their children.

Zhang Xiong, leader of group A of the wild Asian elephant search and monitoring team at the Yunnan Provincial Forest Fire Brigade, was the one who took the picture. Zhang shared that it was a very heartwarming sight.

The baby elephants are just like human children who can't sleep soundly, and they always wake up early. At 9 a.m. one morning, the baby elephant woke up first. It wanted to move around and realized its brothers and sisters were blocking all its ways.

It stepped everywhere on their bodies and tried hard to squeeze out. It climbed and kicked, and kicked again ...

But its young limbs could not wake up the older elephants. Like all human children, the baby elephant had to close its eyes and go back to sleep after a futile effort ...

Zhang said, "The baby elephant kept waving his trunk and tried to climb out after it woke up, but several female elephants tightly surrounded it in the middle. This shows a kind of maternal love."

Elephants Also Like to Chew Unevenly

The baby elephant learned to stand and walk by itself only ten minutes after birth, but it had a harder time learning to make good use of its trunk. How could it eat and drink with its trunk as skillfully as other elephants?

The baby elephant made the first try to drink at the pond but fell directly into it. The mother rushed over and pulled it out with her trunk. So, lesson one for all newcomers to the elephant family is to learn to use their trunks appropriately and give full play to the advantages of their bodies.

After baby elephants are born, they will suck their mother's milk with their mouth. Three months later, some plants will be added to their diet. At this time, they should learn from their mothers how to roll up the grass with their trunks. It takes six months of repeated practice before the baby elephants can skillfully send forage into their mouths with their trunks.

Interestingly, baby elephants have distinct habits. If you look closely, you will see that some of them like to chew their food on the left side of their mouth while others like to chew on the right side.

The journey of the Short Trunks lasted two summers in 2020 and in 2021.

The Elephants Love to Play in the Mud

The dense forests in Yunnan are very hot in summers. The baby elephants were tired of driving away mosquitoes that kept circling around them. The most welcomed thing at these moments would be a mud pond or an irrigation ditch, and the baby elephants would race each other to plunge in. Some chose to slide in from the edge, others jump in between pushing and shoving. It's hard not to fall in love with their innocent playfulness. But don't misunderstand them as being naughty.

Asian elephants have no sweat glands, and their skin is thick with many small seams between their skin folds. A mud bath not only protects them from the sun but also eliminates parasites on their skin and prevents mosquito bites.

Of course, it is much easier to get into the pond than to get out of it. If the baby elephant ran out of energy during the game in a deep muddy pond, it had to call for help from its family. Mom used her trunk to pull and auntie used her butt to push. The baby was finally out of the pond. Just when it started to relax, mom pushed it back into the mud without hesitation. This time, the baby had to learn to climb up by itself.

Was the Elephant Drunk?

In May 2021, the Short Trunks slowly entered Eshan County in Yuxi City.

Then came the "big news" of a young elephant "getting drunk" after greedily foraging for about 200 kg of white distilled liquor and even getting lost from the herd because of oversleeping in the Daweidu village street.

But the relevant departments soon refuted the rumor. The elephant just broke into a human friend's house and drank some liquor. It did not get drunk nor did it lose contact with the herd.

Interestingly, the Short Trunks did show great interest in wine during the journey. Do elephants really like alcohol? How much can they drink?

The truth is, elephants are not good at drinking at all and they can easily get drunk. Their interest in wine is related to their inherited habit of eating fruits. Some fermented fruits produce ethanol, and the smell of ethanol can help them find food.

In short, the young elephants mistook the smell of the residue of distilled spirits for the smell of fruit fermentation. It did not drink the liquor to drink but to eat fruit.

The "Disobedient Child" in the Family

It is said that "a man is a boy until he dies." So is a male elephant. Adult male elephants always seem to retain the nature of a disobedient child and often run counter to the herd, such as running away.

On April 24, 2021, two male elephants separated from the herd in Yuanjiang County, Yuxi City, and returned to Pu'er. They stayed for some time in Mojiang County and Ning'er County, where they ate and bathed in the mountains in the day and toured around the villages at night. On June 5, another male elephant wandered around the villages alone.

Elephants live in a "matriarchal society." The leader of a herd will be the strongest, largest, and oldest female elephant in the family. All other females are related to it. In order to prevent inbreeding, adult males will choose to leave the group when they grow up.

So how do elephants reproduce? This is when male elephants from other families need to intervene.

As for separated elephants, how do they keep in touch with their families if they want to turn back? Elephants have magical communication skills. Due to their constant travel and migration, elephants have developed a long-distance communication technique—infrasound waves (sound waves below 20 Hz, lower than humans can hear). Infrasound waves can travel several kilometers and even more than ten kilometers without interference. Elephants are very smart animals. They know when to make a sound and when it can travel the farthest. Usually at dusk or dawn, when the air is the coldest, the lower temperature makes the sound travel farther.

In addition, if they encounter an emergency or are too far away, they have another communication method that can travel even further distances—feet stamping. The unique soles of elephants' feet save them from squatting down and listening to the vibration of the ground with their ears. Elephants can receive the signals when ground vibrations reach their middle ear from their front feet, leg bones, and shoulder bones. This is one of the reasons why elephants can predict earthquakes.

The Unexpected Uses of Elephant Waste

As we travel along with the Short Trunks, we must mind our steps ... from elephant waste.

Elephants, nature's champion eaters, spend an average of ten hours a day collecting food and eat more than 100 kilograms of food every day. Naturally, the more that goes in, the more that comes out.

Don't underestimate the value of elephant waste. It plays a crucial role in the whole forest ecosystem. For example, insects lay eggs in elephant waste. During hatching, insect larvae provide food for birds or other mammals.

Elephant waste contains many coarse fibers from plants such as bananas. When they decompose, they change back into nutrients for nature. The Asian elephants feed on a wide range of foods. They live in a large habitat and have long migration paths. This way, they bring the seeds over long distances after digesting the plants they eat, which provides favorable conditions for the growth of soil microorganisms.

"Every elephant can create a new world by itself." They are important forest restorers and guardians. Everywhere on the roads they walk by and in the rivers they cross, biodiversity in nature continues to flourish.

Elephants Can Lie Down

Contrary to many people's understandings, the Short Trunks sleep on their backs. In fact, researchers have photographed the Asian elephants lying down and sleeping in Yunnan a few years ago. But in most cases, the Asian elephants stand when they sleep. This is because the adult Asian elephants are too large. If they sleep on their backs for too long, their hearts will be compressed and cause dyspnea (shortness of breath) or even death. In addition, in case of danger, elephants sleeping standing can move quickly and shorten the reaction time of escape. Baby elephants usually sleep lying down. As they grow older and heavier, they will slowly change to sleep standing like other family members.

3

The Elephants Return Home

Although many people hope to hear more stories about the Short Trunks' travel, we all know that they cannot stay out for too long.

From the spring of 2020, the herd was away from home for more than a year touring around Xishuangbanna, Pu'er, Honghe, Yuxi, and Kunming. They had a lot of fun, welcomed new children, and developed a better friendship with mankind … But it was time to go back.

The funny thing is, when the herd began to return south, the "disobedient child" who ran away from the family was "repatriated" first. How was he? What happened to other family members who did not go north with the herd? How were the friends and family in the reserve?

From June 3, 2021, the Short Trunks in the spotlight embarked on the return journey.

Returning South

In early June 2021, the Short Trunks left Kunming and entered Yuxi. On June 17, they entered Eshan County. Here, the herd lingered for four or five days. Maybe they were tired, or maybe they were still looking for a new place to live … The elephants began to move continuously south.

Shen Qingzhong, one of the experts at the provincial headquarters for the security and prevention of Yunnan's northward Asian elephant herd, based on a preliminary judgment suggested that the elephants have shown a tendency of returning to the south, but the specific route still needs to be further studied.

For the elephant-struck crowd, this meant that the magic story of Short Trunks' journey was coming to an end. Many people were disappointed that the "great gathering" of people and elephants in Kunming would not happen. Some netizens joked in the tone of an elephant: "I was planning to see the flag-raising ceremony in Beijing, but I didn't even make it to Kunming. Never mind, I'd better go back home."

Nevertheless, after a year's getting along with the elephants day and night, everyone understands the importance of returning to the south for the Short Trunks.

The return of elephants to the south was a great relief for the "elephant chasers."

The south subtropical region that the wild Asian elephants inhabit often has abundant rainfall, good humidity and heat, and lush plant growth. But where the Short Trunks had reached was already not suitable for Asian elephants to live. If they continued to stay there, their chances of getting ill would increase. Moreover, because there were no other elephant populations in the new region, the Short Trunks may face the danger of extinction due to lack of gene exchanges.

The journey of the Short Trunks benefited from human protection. It was overall a smooth trip despite some ups and downs and exciting events.

In fact, every migration is dangerous and difficult for elephants. For the Short Trunks, the best next stop was home.

From June 22 to 25, the elephants set foot on their return journey and moved south for four consecutive days. They stayed in the woodlands near Fuliangpeng Township, Eshan County, Yuxi City. It seemed that the big family really missed home.

The "Rebellious Boy"

Before we move on to the return journey of the herd, let's take a look at the adolescent male elephant that was "repatriated" first.

On June 26, 2021, the Short Trunks entered Tadian Township in Yuxi City and then moved 4.6 kilometers toward the southeast.

On July 5, the herd entered Xinping County and again moved 16.4 kilometers toward the southeast until they reached the woodlands near Yangwu Township, Xinping County.

On July 8, they detoured 12.6 kilometers and returned south to Longwu Township, Shiping County, Honghe Prefecture the next day.

On July 27, they entered Yuanjiang County through Yangwu County …

The return journey was also long and challenging. But one of the small male elephants arrived home in Mengyang Sub-Reserve when the other members of the family were still on the road.

How did it happen? Did he fly?

The truth was that this young fellow ran away from the family on June 5 and roamed in Kunming after that. But Kunming is not a suitable habitat for Asian elephants, and there isn't so much of the food that wild elephants like. Therefore, the little male elephant went to the villages and "asked" for food from door to door. Sometimes, he ate the food fed by the monitoring staff. But this did not help him grow to be "courteous," and he continued to pay unexpected visits to the neighborhoods in Xiyang Township in Jinning District, Anning City, and Hongta District in Yuxi City, causing much anxiety.

On July 5, this "partying" little male elephant came to Zanbatang community in Beicheng Street in Yuxi City, which is only 0.3 kilometers away from the Jinhong Expressway and 0.2 kilometers away from the Kunyu intercity railway. Considering that it was too close to the transportation network, the public safety risk was too high, and it was difficult for him to return to the elephant herd or return home alone, the provincial headquarters of the elephant protection finally decided to send this "rebellious boy" home ...

In the early morning of July 7, this adolescent male elephant was captured after being anesthetized by the headquarters according to the plan. By 3:00 p.m., he was safely transported back to the habitat. By then, his other family members were still wandering around in Yuxi City.

Across the Yuanjiang River

The successful crossing of the Yuanjiang River Bridge was the most remarkable event in the Short Trunks' return journey.

The Yuanjiang River is one of the oldest rivers in Yunnan, and it is also the division line of two distinctive kinds of vegetation and climates. For the Short Trunks, the south bank was certainly a better habitat.

"Crossing the Yuanjiang River is crucial for the Asian elephants to return to a suitable habitat. Although there is abundant food and water around the Yuanjiang River area, there isn't enough shade or shelter, and it is not good for the elephants to stay for long. When they cross the Yuanjiang River and reach the south bank, their living comfort will be greatly improved, and it will be easier for them to communicate with other herds. It is very meaningful for improving the stability and safety of the species," said Chen Mingyong, an expert on the migrating Asian elephants and professor in the Ecology and Environment Department of Yunnan University.

On May 11, 2020, the Short Trunks crossed the mainstream of the Yuanjiang River and moved north. Two months later, they came to this river again. But it was not the same river as it was ...

Earlier, the elephants crossed the river easily during its dry period. But after the rainy season arrived in July, the water surged and grew violent, making it impossible for the returning the Short Trunks with their youngsters.

From July 27, the Short Trunks were stranded in Yuanjiang and Eshan. Many people wondered why the elephants stopped when they were just a river away from home. Some speculated that it was because the river was swollen and elephants couldn't swim across. Perhaps most people think that animals weighing several tons like elephants will sink. But the elephants—especially the Asian elephants—are actually great swimmers.

They can float easily as long as the water is deep enough, and they do not need to worry about breathing thanks to their long trunks. We rarely see these rainforest inhabitants swim except for crossing rivers during migration. A healthy adult Asian elephant can swim two to three kilometers per hour for five to six hours, so the width of a river doesn't scare them.

So why did the Short Trunks hesitate? It turned out that the elephants were looking for a safe route. While the adult members could possibly swim across the Yuanjiang River in the wet season following the same way, the baby elephants could never make it with the turbulent current that could easily divide the families. So, they could only wait until they found a new way to cross.

Just then, their human friends offered help. To avoid the danger of crossing the river for the elephants, the front-line headquarters set up a route with fences and other security facilities. For thirteen days and twelve nights, they guided the herd through strengthened containment and feeding until they approached the entrance of the Yuanjiang Toll Gate on the Kunming-Mojiang Expressway (linking the northern capital city of Kunming with the southern Mojiang Hani Autonomous County), which led to an old highway bridge to the south bank.

On the evening of August 8, 2021, when the Olympic flame slowly extinguished at the Japan National Stadium, the Short Trunks were walking steadily on the Yuanjiang River Bridge of the G213 highway. Their huge figures gradually disappeared into the night that fell upon the south bank.

"It was impossible for elephants to use the bridge before! But these elephants have chosen their way home arranged by humans ..." The monitoring team of

Yunnan Provincial Forest Fire Brigade found the event very exciting. It showed that elephants understood that humans meant no harm.

Getting Ready to Go Home

It was a big step for the Short Trunks to cross the mainstream of the Yuanjiang River and return to their suitable habitat, but this was not the end of the journey yet.

On August 12, 2021, the Tenth World Elephant Day, the Short Trunks finally entered Mojiang County in Pu'er City, which was very close to their home in Xishuangbanna. But the herd stopped again for twenty-one days. Their favorite fresh, juicy corn had ripened, and they also found rich forage thanks to Mojiang County's increasing efforts in ecological protection in recent years. Feeling "obliged" to enjoy the delicious food, the Short Trunks started feasting and partying in Mojiang.

Living leisurely in a comfortable habitat with plenty of food must be the dream life of every elephant. Apparently, the Short Trunks were in no hurry to go home anymore. All the family members had probably put on some weight during their stay in Mojiang, and the babies clearly grew stronger and more energetic.

After this precious "holiday," the elephants continued on their way home. At 1:40 a.m. on September 1, the staff guided the Short Trunks to cross the Guozhe Bridge over the Amo River and into Jingxing Township. From there, they began the last journey toward their original habitat 100 kilometers away.

Now, the home was right in front of them. The Short Trunks' steps became slower and gentler. The mother held her baby with her trunk to lead it forward, just like human parents holding the hands of their own children. Many times, we saw the mother "whispering" to the baby as if telling it about the beautiful home it had not yet seen. They were ready to go home.

All's Well

Today, we are still thinking about the Short Trunks. How is life back home? Are they happy? Are they comfortable? Don't worry. They are enjoying every lazy afternoon with the beautiful sunlight in Xishuangbanna. Now they are at home and are often busy with all the dinner plans with their besties and buddies.

The safe return of the wild Asian elephants in Yunnan is a victory of public protection of elephants and a manifestation of harmonious coexistence between man and nature. For us, the story of the Short Trunks shouldn't end after their return. Rather, it should only grow to be more exciting as we continue to love and protect them and their elephant friends in the future.

According to the monitoring team members, the elephants are in good condition in all aspects. They have gained quite a lot of weight during their trip with all the exercising, eating, and sleeping. The two baby elephants born on the way to the north are also growing fast and healthily. Now that they had settled down in a relatively stable environment, they began to be braver too. The once timid little fellows always hiding at their mother's side are now daring to act alone. They often run a little away from their mothers to look for food alone before running back to the herd. Clearly, the young elephants have made remarkable progress in their physiological functions and living skills.

The herd is not afraid of strangers anymore. The local villagers are already used to the frequent visits of elephants. As for the elephants, they know the residents there like old friends. The Short Trunks are still making routine travel plans to the villages where they usually stay for several days. But they never have to worry about what to eat because there are always plenty of choices everywhere. The villages they have been to are also famous now. Some people even made holiday reservations to enjoy the leisure and comfortable rural life.

CALENDAR OF THE SHORT TRUNKS' JOURNEY

The Northbound Route

April 16, 2021
The herd entered Yuanjiang County, Yuxi City from Mojiang County, Pu'er City.

May 16, 2021
The herd entered Shiping County, Honghe Prefecture from Yuanjiang County, Yuxi City.

May 24, 2021
The herd entered Eshan County, Yuxi City from Shiping County, Honghe Prefecture.

May 27, 2021
The herd crossed Eshan Township.

May 29, 2021
The herd entered Hongta District from Eshan County.

June 2, 2021
The herd entered Jinning District, Kunming City from Hongta District, Yuxi City.

The Solo Elephant's Route

June 5, 2021
The solo elephant left the herd.

July 7, 2021
The solo elephant was returned to the habitat safely.

The Southbound Route

June 8, 2021
The herd entered Yimen County.

June 17, 2021
The herd entered Eshan County.

July 5, 2021
The herd entered Xinping County, Yuxi City.

July 9, 2021
The herd entered Eshan County.

July 10, 2021
The herd entered Shiping County.

July 27, 2021
The herd entered Yuanjiang County.

August 8, 2021
The herd crossed the mainstream of the Yuanjiang River through the Yuanjiang River Bridge.

August 23, 2021
The herd stayed in the woodland on the east of Lianglu Village, Lianzhu Township, Mojiang County.

♀ Ning'er County

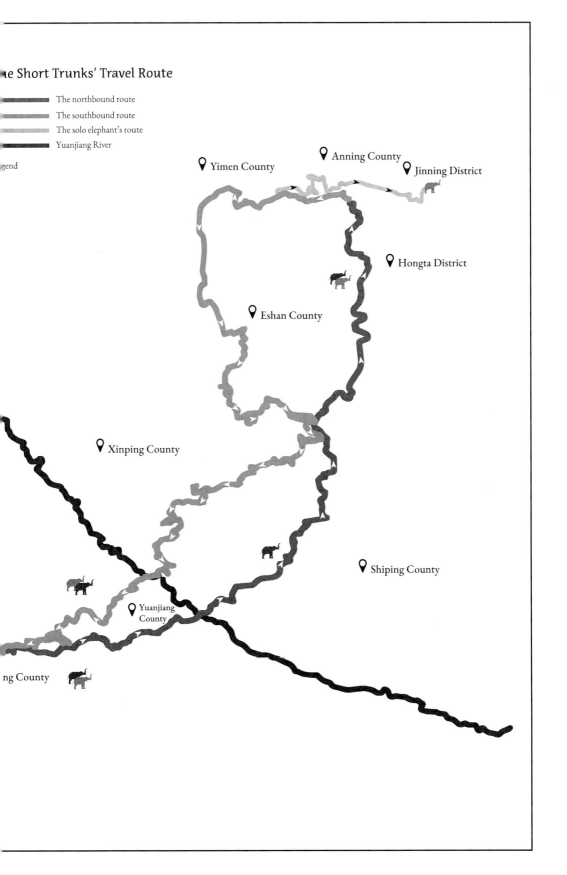

The Short Trunks' Travel Route

Yimen County

Anning County

Jinning District

Hongta District

Eshan County

Xinping County

Shiping County

Yuanjiang County

ng County

4

Stories of Life Together

There are too many things we talk about of the journey of the Short Trunks that has now come to an end. We remember all the cute and hilarious moments, and we also remember the ecological significance of this incident.

What deserves mentioning the most—what makes all these values possible— is the fact that no elephant or person was injured during the entire process. It contains many people's meticulous care and efforts as well as the elephants' kind willingness to behave in a gentle and friendly manner. Both sides have conveyed their good intentions to the greatest level, which is proof of China's healthy and harmonious ecological civilization.

Nothing is more important than keeping everyone safe. Certainly, a careful review of how this was done will have profound implications for dealing with similar incidents around the world.

The "Sweet Trouble"

The truth is that elephant migration can be very risky and dangerous. They may run into serious problems with food and water supply on the way, and the possible human-elephant conflict is even more concerning. Fortunately, the people in Yunnan adore elephants, and they also know how to protect them. No one takes the Short Trunks' travel as a repulsive offense. It was at worst considered "sweet trouble." The elephants have indeed had a certain impact on local people's lives. Elephants that live around human communities are "immune" to the crowd. They often hang out in the fields or drink from the farmhouse reservoir. Sometimes, to make way for the elephants, people have to stop their work and stay indoors. But even so, the people of Yunnan never complain.

"The elephants are in my field."

"The elephants came to my house to drink last night."

"How lucky you are!"

"Why didn't the elephants come to my house?"

No one blames the elephants for their mischief. The elephants are their guests, and it is only decent that the host serves their guests well.

"It's not like they are here every day; what does it matter if they want to eat a little bit more? Let them eat if they want to." Some people even cut down a whole cart of plantain from their fields to give to the elephants. Mrs. Tang Zhengfang in Jinning was so excited when she heard that the elephants were coming to her village. Fearing that the elephants may not have enough to eat after walking a long way, she reached out to the Township government and donated her own corn to feed the elephants.

It was just in time of the Kuzhazha Festival for the Hani people when the Short Trunks arrived.[1] But they canceled the celebration in order not to disturb the elephants. Instead, they put up "lucky elephant" slogans to send their blessings for peace and harmony between humans and elephants.

Thanks to their kind and helpful human neighbors, the Short Trunks were very well received and supported throughout their journey.

---

1. Kuzhazha Festival, also called the "June New Year," is an important traditional festival for the Hani ethnic people in Yunnan. On this day, people drink, feast, play music, and dance throughout the night.

"We Didn't Dare to Move"

The Short Trunks get along well with people, but we must not ignore their huge size and the danger they are capable of causing because of their cuteness. The premise of harmonious coexistence between humans and elephants is to keep an absolutely safe distance from each other.

Once, the elephants slowly entered a village at night and carefully inspected the surroundings. The elephant in the lead was very alert. After she confirmed the safety of the route, the herd followed. The villagers had already received a warning of the elephants' arrival and had taken shelter on the second floor of two solid brick buildings. Food that the elephants liked, such as corn and salt, had also been safely stored away. The sudden visit of the elephants was both exciting and terrifying for the villagers.

One of them recalled: "We did not dare make any sound when the elephants passed by. We felt the road shaking when those fifteen giants walked toward us. They could nearly reach us on the second floor when they raised their trunks. We didn't dare to move, just hid silently upstairs." After the elephants left, a villager found his gate squashed and his kitchen and warehouse in a mess.

This is an example of people's direct contact with elephants. Getting too close to the elephants or provoking them will lead to unimaginable consequences. For many people in Yunnan, the story ended perfectly both for the elephants and for humans especially since no one was hurt.

Prevent Human-Elephant Conflict

Yunnan Province has rich experience in avoiding human-elephant conflicts. As early as in 1998, Yunnan promulgated the Measures for Compensation for Personal and Property Damage Caused by Key Protected Terrestrial Wild Animals in Yunnan Province, which included the funds required for compensation into the budgets of governments at all levels. In 2009, the Xishuangbanna Asian Elephant Public Liability Insurance Service Agreement tried to introduce for the first time in Xishuangbanna a commercial insurance mechanism to compensate for the losses caused by wild elephant accidents. It was the first insurance policy in China to include wildlife accident insurance into commercial insurance compensation, and the transformation from government compensation to commercial compensation was gradually realized. Between 2014 and 2020, a total of 173 million RMB was compensated for the losses due to the accidents of Asian elephants.

We have learned a lot from living together with the elephants for many years. For example, the journey of the Short Trunks proved that elephants must "eat well," which inspires the subsequent construction of the elephant provenance base and national parks; in addition, we see that elephants can understand human kindness since they will gladly accept the help provided by people.

Why Do Elephants Live in Herds?

"Cattle and sheep flock together, while wild beasts always walk alone." This idiom implies that the powerful have the courage to move forward alone, while the weak can only live together for survival. As the largest and certainly powerful mammal on land, why do elephants choose to live in herds? Are they afraid of danger or loneliness? Actually, the social habits of elephants cannot be attributed simply to safety or warmth. Elephants are animals with complex social habits. Living in groups is not only beneficial for avoiding danger but also for the division of labor, foraging, joint defense, joint education of young elephants, increasing mating opportunities, and so on.

A typical elephant family usually has five to twenty members consisting of two to three adult female elephants and their offspring, or an elderly elephant, one to two adult female elephants, and their offspring. The other members are often females who are also related. In human society, grandparents often help their children with babysitting and impart their wisdom in raising offspring. This pattern also applies to other social mammals such as dolphins, whales, and elephants. Therefore, the elephant herd is generally led by an experienced elderly female member who is responsible for all the decisions of the family. Everyone in the family acts under the command of the leader.

The elephant family members share a very close relationship. The female elephants are very devoted to raising their children. All the females will take turns to take care of each other's calves, and some will even feed children that are not theirs. We can see the deep-rooted family values of elephant herds. The baby elephants receive the most care and attention in the group. If the baby elephant falls behind, the mother will wait for it; when the baby elephant screams, every member of the herd will respond; if the baby elephant falls down, the mother will help it up ...

When a female baby elephant reaches maturity, she will remain in the family and breed the next generation; but young males usually leave the herd when he grows up to about twelve years old. This is not because the family wants to abandon it but because the young male needs to find his own spouse. He can't "marry" within the herd because the female members are all relative to him. But although these young males and the new sub-herds they later form are separated from the family, they continue to interact in a cooperative way. Two to four sub-herds related by blood often live and carry out daily activities close together.

Elephants are highly intelligent animals, so their relationship and interactions in social activities are very complex. Like humans, they have their own emotional lives and social etiquette. When they greet each other, they put the tip of their trunks into the other elephant's mouth and then touch and lean on each other. When separated elephants reunite, they perform a more complicated greeting including the excited flapping of ears and the making of low-pitched rumbling noises. This means that they welcome the other member's return. If one of the members of the family experiences discomfort and behaves agitated or abnormal, the others will rush over to help by patting gently with their trunks. In extreme situations, several adult elephants will stand in a circle and protect their family member in distress inside.

Such social connections among the members of the elephant herd can last for life. From them, we see precious characteristics that human beings are born with and highly value but are slowly losing in complex social life. Maybe this is why elephants can arouse so much affection in us.

5

The Friends and Family of the Short Trunks

As the Short Trunks returned to their hometown and the story of their travel spread, the world grew more and more interested in Xishuangbanna, the hometown of the elephants. People are curious about the reason why the elephants went north, how they interacted with humans, and how many wild Asian elephants are living in the rainforest in Yunnan ...

The Asian elephants in China are distributed in Xishuangbanna, Pu'er, Lincang, and other regions in Yunnan Province, and 90% of the population is in Xishuangbanna. In recent years, ecological environment protection measures in China have quickly developed, and the forestation coverage rate of Xishuangbanna National Nature Reserve has increased from 88.9% in the 1980s to 97.02% now. These efforts have enabled more living space for Asian elephants. Today, there are around 300 wild Asian elephants in several herds in Yunnan reserves. Many new elephant herds, like the Short Trunks, are originally from one large family.

In 2006, the Xishuangbanna Wild Elephant Valley set up an Asian elephant observation and protection team. Shortly thereafter, the team members found a one-year-old baby elephant with a short trunk in the herd. She was named Little Short Trunk. Her mother was a strong, loving female elephant. When Little Short Trunk was five years old, her mother gave her a new baby sister. Little Short Trunk also had a close older sister, Blue Eyes.

When elephant communities expand, big families are usually dispersed and reorganized. In 2015, Little Short Trunk was ten years old, and she was becoming more and more independent. But she was still too young to leave her mother. Most of the time, she lived with her big sister. But in the following years later, she also stayed with the large family of the Big Humps.

The leader of the Big Humps has humps on both her shoulders. That's how the herd was named.[2] The old female leader is over fifty years old and has a lot of life experiences, and her family which consists of twenty members is also the largest that the Wild Elephant Valley has ever had. In spite of their advantage in numbers, the Big Humps never pick on other families with fewer members. They don't mind if others want to share the nitrite pond. The old matriarch is kind and loving; her family members are also at peace and inclusive. This attracted many teenage elephants from other families. Among them were Little Short Trunk and her childhood playmate Spotted Trunk. Later, Spotted Trunk formed her own family, and Little Short Trunk went with them. But she never forgot about her own sister Blue Eyes. When Blue Eyes had her calf at the beginning of 2018, Little Short Trunk returned to her and helped to take care of her nephew.

The year 2020 was an extraordinary year. Little Short Trunk was fifteen, and now she was almost fully grown. At the beginning of the year, about eighty Asian elephants were gathering in the Wild Elephant Valley. Soon afterward, fifteen of them including Little Short Trunk, Blue Eyes, and Spotted Trunk formed their own herd. They began to move northward from Xishuangbanna. Sometime later, an adult male elephant joined in and made up the sixteenth member of the herd. This then became the Short Trunks' epic journey that attracted worldwide attention.

Another elephant family in the Reserve worth mentioning is the Ranrans. In July 2005, the Xishuangbanna Prefecture rescued a young female elephant injured by a trap near the observatory. She was named Ranran, and so the herd that she was in was also named the Ranran family.

---

2. The Big Humps are also called Da Lubaos in Xishuangbanna's local dialect.

The Ranrans are generally tall, with long legs, a round head, and a pair of heart-shaped ears. This is also a large family with more than fifteen members, led by two highly respected old female elephants. Unlike the others, the Ranrans like gatherings. They pay the most visits to the human villages. They also have strong mobility. Many of them have joined other herds. Members of elephant herds are often exchanged. Many new herds are formed centering "sister groups" or "bestie groups." Adult male elephants often drop by during the mating season every year. Baby Bamboo Teeth is a famous celebrity in Wild Elephant Valley.

In 2016, during the Spring Festival, the young and ruthless Baby Bamboo Teeth fell in love with the second daughter in the Ranran family, and he even challenged the strongest adult elephant Big Teeth in the Valley trying to win her over. But of course, he lost the fight. Angry and depressed, he wandered around and vented his rage on the tourists' vehicles. Nineteen automobiles were damaged in three days. Since then, he became famous as the "lovelorn elephant" and drew a lot of attention on the Internet.

There is another adult male elephant in the Valley called Fat Neck. He is softer and gentler. Unlike the young and vigorous Baby Bamboo Teeth, Fat Neck never bullies the weak. Adult male elephants are often grumpy and can sometimes be very impatient with the naughty young elephants, even Big Teeth who is highly welcomed among the females. But Fat Neck is very patient with the babies. Once, he even took over the responsibility of the mother elephant and kept the baby elephant by his side. They dined quietly together, and Fat Neck caressed the baby with his trunk from time to time like a loving old father. His calm and gentle character impressed many female elephants, and many chose to follow him.

When the Short Trunks were under the spotlight, another elephant family with seventeen members also left their habitat Mengyang Sub-Reserve. The leader of this family is a female elephant in her 30s with ears full of little nicks. This family was thus named the Little Nicked Ears. They traveled slowly with seven young elephants. On their way, they broke into the Xishuangbanna Tropical Botanical Garden of the Chinese Academy of Sciences in Mengla County. Later, the river rose during the rainy season. The Little Nicked Ears failed to cross the river after many attempts and stayed in the Botanical Garden for some time.

After the Short Trunks returned to the south, some experts pointed out that the elephants' northbound journeys may still occur in the future. This is not what humans want to see. We are facing major problems with protecting biodiversity, improving the environmental quality of the Asian elephant habitat in Xishuangbanna, and meeting the growing needs of elephant populations for habitat. Nevertheless, we are convinced of a promising future of lives together. We look forward to seeing Xishuangbanna accommodating more wild Asian elephants and becoming a proud "elephant haven."

6

Things You May Not Know about Wild Elephants

What Are the Differences between Asian Elephants and African Elephants?

There are two kinds of elephants: Asian elephants and African elephants. Some scholars also believe that there are four subspecies of Asian elephants—Indian elephants, Sri Lankan elephants, Sumatran elephants, and Borneo Elephants—as well as two subspecies of African elephants—African forest elephants and African grassland elephants. In recent years, with the deepening of research, the African forest elephant, once considered as a subspecies, has been identified as an independent species juxtaposed with the Asian elephant and the African grassland elephant.

We can easily distinguish between Asian elephants and African elephants from their appearances. African elephants have very large ears, sometimes even larger than their faces, with an outline that resembles the African continent. The Asian elephants have smaller ears that look like the Indian peninsula. African elephants have two "convex nostrils" at the tip of their trunks, while Asian elephants have only one. People can also judge from their tusks. Both male and female African elephants have exposed tusks, while only some male Asian elephants have tusks.

Geographically, African elephants mainly live in the humid tropical forests in central and west Africa below the Sahara Desert as well as in the deserts of Mali. Asian elephants mainly live in shrublands and rainforests in Nepal, India, and Southeast Asia. In China, they are only distributed in Xishuangbanna, Pu'er, Lincang, and other regions in the south of Yunnan Province.

Elephants Are Champion Eaters

The daily life of elephants is basically occupied by only one thing—eating. Elephants are pure herbivores. Each elephant needs hundreds of kilograms of food a day, which is equivalent to 6% to 8% of the elephant's body weight.

Grass, shrubs, fruits, twigs, bark, and roots are all part of their diet. Sometimes, elephants also eat soil to obtain salt and minerals. Human crops such as corn, rice, peanuts, bananas, jackfruit, coconut, etc., are also in favor. It is a lot easier to find enough nutritious food in the fields than in the wild, where they have to forage by themselves.

Elephants eat continuously for most of the day. Therefore, the quantity of food they can access is crucial for their survival and determines their migration.

Why Do Elephants Have Such Long Trunks?

The elephant trunk is the most sensitive organ of mammals on earth. The trunk is actually a combination of an elephant's upper lip and nose. It is composed of 150,000 muscle tissues with a finger-shaped bulge at the end. It is powerful enough to lift objects weighing up to hundreds of kilograms and flexible enough to peel off the shells of peanuts. Elephants use their trunks to drink too. There is a structure similar to a "valve" in their trunks. When drawing water, the "valve" will automatically close to prevent water from entering the trachea or lungs. The trunk can hold up to eight liters of water at a time. When swimming, elephants use their trunks as breathing tubes.

Elephant tusks evolve from front teeth. This process can be observed most clearly when elephants are about two years old. Elephants' tusks continue to grow throughout their lives, and thus the huge tusks are also a sign of prestige and status. They are also of practical importance such as for peeling barks, digging roots, digging earth, or gathering food on the ground during foraging or for protection in battles.

Like people who can be left-handed or right-handed, elephants also have their habitual side of the tusks. It is easy to tell: the side that is worn out more is the side they prefer to use.

Elephants have very thick (an average of 2.5 cm) and wrinkled skin that can store ten times more water than the flat skin does. This helps keep the body cool. Elephants like to "bathe" in mud and sand. This is also a self-protection measure. The soil attached to the body can not only prevent mosquito bites but also avoid excessive sun exposure.

These intelligent animals have a lot of clever tricks like this. Studies have shown that the average IQ of elephants is equivalent to that of human children aged four to five. Moreover, because the temporal lobe of the elephant brain (the brain area related to memory) is larger and denser than human beings, elephants have better long-term memories and can remember migration routes from decades ago and the exact location of each food and water source.

The intelligence of elephants is comparable to that of chimpanzees and other highly intelligent animals. They know how to use tree branches to drive away flies and block the water holes with chewed tree barks to prevent them from drying up. Elephants are good at cooperative problem-solving. For example, after observing the rules of an experiment, elephants can quickly understand that they need help from a partner to get food.

In addition, elephants also have a high degree of compassion and strong emotional bonds with each other. They will comfort companions who are defeated or injured and mourn for deaths in families. When they encounter the skeleton of another elephant, they will slow down, approach it, and caress the bones with their sensitive trunks and soles. They only show such interest in the remains of their own kind. Scientists have also seen elephants kicking dirt onto the corpse of their companions and covering them with palm leaves.

Elephants Are Social Butterflies

Elephants reach sexual maturity between the ages of ten and twelve. Male elephants will leave the herd as long as they can find food and protect themselves. Adult males generally live alone. If living with a herd, they only assume the responsibility of protecting the safety of the group. Therefore, the elephant herd operates according to the principle of "matriarchal society," and the head of the herd is usually the oldest female. The elephant communities can split up and reform. A female elephant often forms a herd with her offspring or related females, and the number is usually between six and twenty. When the family becomes too big or comes across difficulty in foraging, the herd will divide into smaller groups.

Most of the time, the separated elephant sub-herd will stay in the same habitat area. But every herd is different. Some are more adventurous than others. Asian elephants are not technically forest species, and they prefer open space. If a major change takes place in their current habitats, such as climate change or a food shortage, some special herds may reactivate their instinct to roam the vast territory where their ancestors once lived, looking for new food sources and habitats. Because of their swarming characteristic, "social" is very important for elephants.

Elephants communicate in a variety of ways, including sound, body language, physical interaction, and smell. In addition to the loud trumpet-like roars and many different kinds of snorting, crooning, barking, and growling, elephants can also send out sound waves with a low frequency that cannot be heard by humans. This low infrasound wave can travel 20 kilometers away.

In the eyes of humans, the folding of ears and stepping back of elephants may seem to be meaningless, but they are actually part of the important body language system of elephants. Elephants show aggression and intimidation by stretching their ears, standing upright, and raising their tusks. They gently nod their heads to show joy. They greet each other by holding up their trunks high or putting the end of their trunk in the mouth of another elephant.

Elephants have a very sensitive sense of smell that can help them identify the smell of urine and feces left by their companions during long journeys so as to keep up with the herd as soon as possible.

Some experts believe that elephants have a more fantastic way of communication—they stamp their feet regularly on the ground to create the vibration, which is then perceived by other elephants with their soles and transmitted to the inner ear through bones. They communicate in this way to transmit danger signals or information about water and food sources when herds are far away and blocked by natural barriers.

Cute Elephants Can Be Dangerous

Elephants have always been liked for their honest look, smart character, and gentle personality. Many lovable cartoon characters such as Dumbo from the Disney film and Emily from *Peppa Pig* capture and highlight these features very well.

In traditional Chinese culture, elephants are seen as "spiritual beasts" with good omens such as auspiciousness and longevity. Therefore, when the Short Trunks' long journey caught the public's eyes, the common reactions were joy and excitement. People thought the elephants were cute, and there were even some romantic interpretations of their migration. But the danger of these elephants was generally overlooked. These giant animals can easily enter the realm of humans because ordinary roads and fences cannot stop them. As wild animals, elephants retain their natural wildness and have less experience in living with humans. The human-elephant encounters can be extremely dangerous if the elephant is frightened and takes defensive actions.

In 2017, a wild elephant entered a village in Odisha (formerly Orissa), India. Excited onlookers gathered around it to take photos. Stimulated by the flash of the mobile phones, the angry elephant attacked the villagers who approached it for selfies by rolling its trunk and trampling with its feet. This shows the danger of interacting with wild elephants that can easily behave aggressively. Therefore, when traveling on routes that elephants may pass through, it is important not to expose food that may attract elephants. When encountering an elephant, quickly avoid the area and keep a safe distance from the elephant. Never approach, tease, block, or chase the elephant without authorization so as to avoid scaring or annoying them.

CHAPTER 2

A New Look for a New World

"Actively serve and merge into the national development strategy, create a path of leaping forward development, strive to become a demonstration area of national unity and progress, the leader in the construction of an ecological civilization, and a radiating center facing South and Southeast Asia, and write the story of Yunnan in achieving the Chinese Dream."

—From Secrectary-General Xi Jinping's important talk during his visit to Yunnan in January 2015.

"It is hoped that Yunnan will correctly understand and take advantage of its role in the overall national development, resolutely implement the major decisions and arrangements of the CPC Central Committee, comprehensively promote the work of stabilizing growth, promoting reform, adjusting structure, benefiting people's livelihoods, preventing risks, and ensuring stability, striving to make new progress in building China's demonstration area of national unity and progress, the leader of ecological civilization construction, and the radiating center facing South and Southeast Asia Exhibition, and write the story of Yunnan in achieving the Chinese Dream."

—From Secrectary-General Xi Jinping's important talk during his visit to Yunnan in January 2020.

In 2015 and 2020, Secrectary-General Xi Jinping visited Yunnan twice and encouraged Yunnan to become a leader in the construction of an ecological civilization and continue to make new progress. Under the guidance of his idea of an ecological civilization, Yunnan promoted the construction of an ecological civilization with unprecedented determination and force on the "three major defense wars" of blue sky, clear water, and clean soil with improving the quality of an ecological environment as the core. Gratifying results were achieved, and the story of the Short Trunks and other Asian elephants is the most vivid epitome.

1

A Two-Thousand-Year Friendship

The friendship of people in Yunnan and elephants can be traced back to 2,000 years ago in written records alone. It was written in *Records of the Grand Historian: Biography of Dayuan*: "There are no kings or lords in the multiple nomad clans of Kunming. Bandits and thieves were rampant, and they always murdered or robbed Chinese envoys. We haven't been able to pass through this region. However, it is said that several thousand *li* to the west, there is an elephant-riding kingdom called Dianyue."

Dianyue refers to the region between Baoshan City and the Dehong Dai and Jingpo Autonomous Prefecture in modern Yunnan Province. The center of this region might have been in Tengchong City, or what was called Tengyue in ancient times. The elephant-riding kingdom, of course, means a kingdom where people rode on elephants. Even today, many people from other provinces still like to joke on the Yunnan locals: "Do you ride elephants to school?"

There is plenty of evidence of the history of elephants as part of people's lives in ancient Yunnan (Dian). They were not only an important means of transportation but also indispensable helpers in farming. The multiple roles that elephants played reflect the most typical characteristics of the "elephant farming" culture. Moreover, domesticated elephants could also be used in combat. According to historical records, Kublai Khan went on an expedition in an elephant chariot in the Yuan Dynasty (1271–1368 AD). The poet Wei Chu (1232–1292 AD) even wrote, "After the emperor opened up Yunnan with his horsewhip, we finally have an elephant in the central plains" to memorialize these exotic animals.

Elephants were often trained for wars in Yunnan, and they proved to be very brave and powerful fighters. The vivid description of Meng Huo fighting on an elephant in the classic book *Romance of the Three Kingdoms*, for example, leaves a deep impression on many readers. In the Ming (1368–1644 AD) and Qing (1636–1912 AD) dynasties, elephants were put in the front row of imperial ritual ceremonies. They were mostly imported from southern neighboring countries as tributes, and they had to pass through Yunnan on their way north. Especially in the Qing Dynasty, tributary elephants were sent to Beijing every three to five years through Kunming. At that time, the little rest that the elephants took at Kunming was a favorite topic of the local residents, and the elephant bathing was also the city's most splendid celebration every summer. We can still imagine the incredible scene of elephants bathing in the Panlong River from a Ming dynasty poem: "The banks of the Panlong River are covered by the shades of lush pagoda trees and filled with luxurious chariots and elegant sedans. People spent fortunes on a seat by the window, just to get a better view of the bathing elephants."

The northward migration of the Short Trunks brought Asian elephants in Yunnan to Shuanghe Township, Jinning District, Kunming, which was the northernmost place that has been recorded. This wonderful surprise also brought painful sentiments. These elephants that now seem to originate from Yunnan were once "indigenous residents" in northern China. They were widely distributed on both sides of the Yangtze River and as far as the Yellow River Basin. However, with the changes in the natural environment and the impact of human production and life, the elephant habitat retreated further and further to the south, until Yunnan became their only home in China. This beautiful, intelligent creature has bravely endured the hardships of time and survived in a narrower and narrower space. It is true that before the amazing story of the Short Trunks has created a sensation in the world, we were more used to hearing provocative news of elephants being hurt by humans.

These giant, powerful, and fierce beasts listed as an endangered species in the International Union for Conservation of Nature (IUCN)'s red list are so fragile and vulnerable in front of human beings. But things are different for them now in China with a harmonious coexistence between humans and nature. In Yunnan, the treasury of biodiversity, elephants are living a safe and peaceful life.

Yunnan not only maintained an environment suitable for elephants with lush forests, deep valleys, and a wide range of species but also made huge efforts in protecting the Asian elephants, including protecting and developing their habitats, cracking down on hunting and illegal trade, constructing the "elephant provenance base," and implementing "green tunnels." Since the 1980s and 90s, the number of wild Asian elephants in Yunnan has increased from around 180 to 300 today.

We may even say that after at least two thousand years of life together, the love for elephants has already become part of the cultural genes of the Yunnan people. Take the Short Trunks as an example. Their northbound journey has indeed caused a lot of trouble to local people's daily lives, but people smiled at their "mistakes" as if when dealing with clumsy children. Said the simple and affectionate local villagers, "It's ok, just let them eat. Our crops can still grow next year, but elephants won't come back if they die out."

More than Twenty-Five Genera of Wild Elephants Lived in Yunnan

More ancient than the written records is the fossil evidence. According to Ji Xueping, a researcher at the Yunnan Institute of Cultural Relics and Archaeology, incomplete statistics show that Yunnan used to be the habitat for more than 25 genera of ancient elephants. It is the origin of many vertebrates and a "refuge" for many ancient species, including Asian elephants.

Based on the ice age theory, Ji explained that: "Due to the interaction between outer space and the earth, the earth will complete an alternation of warm periods and ice ages every other cycle. The arrival of the ice age leads to the migration of ancient elephants to places with mild climate and lush vegetation. From the fossils unearthed, ancient elephants chose Yunnan many times in their migrations."

"Fossil evidence of ancient and extinct elephant-like creatures are widely distributed in Yunnan, and many of them are named after the places they were discovered in Yunnan for the first time." Ji provided the following timeline:

Around 12 million years ago, Stegolophodon, Zygolophodon chinjiensis, and Gomphotherium xiaolongtanensis lived in today's Xiaolongtan Township, Kaiyuan City;

Around 8 million years ago, Lufeng zygolophodon and Gomphotherium lived in today's Lufeng region;

Around 7.2 million to 8.2 million years ago, Zhupeng zygolophodon, Xiaohe tetralophodon, Jiangyi stegotetrabelodon, Sinomastodon, Banguo stegolophodon, Primitive stegodon and others lived in today's Yuanmou region;

Around 6.5 million to 6 million years ago, Zhaotong stegodon, Sinomastodon preintermedius, Sawtooth-like gomphotherium, Rhynchotherium huananensis, Zygolophodon chinjiensis, Tetralophodon and others lived in today's Zhaotong region;

Around six million years ago, Baoshan stegodon, Sinomastodon, and Changning stegodon lived in today's Baoshan region, and Zhaotong stegodon lived in the Kunming Basin ...

When and how did these ancient species extinct? About six million years ago, the global climate turned dry and cold. The species in Yunnan suffered from a sharp decline, and elephants were also among that mass extinction.

"But Primitive stegodon (equivalent to Zhaotong stegodon or Stegodon zdanskyi) and Gomphotherium survived in the Yuanmou Basin. About 1.7 million years ago, new groups of Stegodon appeared, namely the Yuanmou stegodon, Stegodon elephantoides, and so on. In the same period, in today's Yongren area, there were the Stegodon preorientalis and Yongren gomphotherium. Since then, the species and number of elephants have greatly decreased. Only the Stegodon orientalis remained and coexisted with ancient humans, giant pandas, and other animals. Around 20,000 to 30,000 years ago, some Stegodons in South China moved south to Southeast Asia. The geographical isolation of the island dwarfed their body and reduced their height to about 1.5 meters. The Stegodons that lived mainly on leaves were unable to adapt to the changes of their habitat and eventually became extinct around 10,000 years ago," said Ji.

So, when did the Asian elephant appear in Yunnan?

Ji explained that Asian elephant fossils have been widely found in the middle and late Pleistocene strata in South China and in the south of the Yellow River Basin, coexisting with Stegodon orientalis for a long time. However, fossil records of ancient Asian elephants and Asian elephants are only found in a few locations such as Zhaotong and Fumin in Yunnan.

Asian elephants survived because of their ability to adapt to a variety of food resources and habitats. However, the dual influences of climate change and human activities are forcing Asian elephants to retreat further south. Now, they only live in Yunnan's subtropical forests below the altitude of 1,000 meters in Xishuangbanna, Pu'er, and Lincang.

Elephants in Ancient Poems

Seeing the Elephant

After the emperor opened up Yunnan with his horsewhip,

We finally had an elephant in the central plain.

There have been legends, but no one has ever seen one.

Everyone rushed to see it, and the animal shocks us like a thunderbolt.

Its huge trunk is six or seven feet long,

Swaying and rolling from left to right to send food to its mouth.

Its ears and neck are the size of several oxen,

Its skin and fur are the color of the black boar.

Its eyes sparkle like mirrors,

Its back is expansive, like mountain crags.

The curly-haired barbarians make iron into weapons

And intend to drive the elephants to disturb us.

But I hear that our country values the virtuous and the talented,

And so all exotic beings come without being forced.

If someone can write a eulogy about the mastiff dogs from the west

Sent in as a tribute, the fame of our country will definitely last and spread.

—Wei Chu, Yuan Dynasty (1271–1368 AD)

Trip Along the River in Lingnan

The Zhangjiang River flows south into the clouds.

The *huangmao* plants cover the land up to the sea.

The sun shines after the rain, and elephants appear on the hillside.

The sun warms up the pond, and leeches come out in the water.

The lurking monster is secretly prying into the traveler's footsteps,

And the hurricane-forewarning rainbow

Is suddenly bringing shocks to the visitor's boats.

From now on, so many duties are ahead of me.

How can I waste my time away, while my hair is already grey?

—Liu Zongyuan, Tang Dynasty (618–907 AD)

The Place They Met

The place they met, under a clear evening sky,

Was in front of the ancient King Yue's terrace

Below the Indian coral blossoms.

Secretly, she turned her eyes and looked back at him.

Such deep affection!

She dropped her green hairpins,

But quickly crossed the river on her elephant.

—Li Xun, Five Dynasties and Ten Kingdoms Period (907–979 AD)

2

Tips on Elephant Protection from Yunnan

Today, Yunnan is a paradise for Asian elephants. They can find abundant food and water there and do not need to worry about poaching. In their own "amusement park," the natural reserves, their population is growing steadily.

As mentioned in the previous chapter, two baby elephants were born during the Short Trunks' journey. It follows then that Yunnan has done a good job in protecting Asian elephants.

Today, about 300 wild Asian elephants live in Yunnan. Although this number is not large enough to remove them from the "endangered" list, it has doubled in number in the twentieth century. Back then, the population of Asian elephants in Yunnan showed a continuous downward trend. Asian elephants have few natural enemies, but that doesn't mean they can survive easily. Accidental injuries, infections, and diseases can all be life-threatening. More importantly, Asian elephants faced the problems of narrow and scattered distribution areas, declining habitat quality, and decreasing population genetic diversity, and were once on the verge of extinction. To save this species, Yunnan has spent years on elephant habitat construction, monitoring and early warning, food source protection, and rescue. Finally, through decades of efforts, the population of Asian elephants in Yunnan continues to grow. We also met the Ranran and Short Trunks families that later became famous.

The Pro in Elephant Protection

What has Yunnan done specifically to protect Asian elephants? What experience is worth learning from?

The first and foremost contribution is to severely crack down on poaching and illegal trade. For a long time, hunting was allowed in Yunnan's deep, vibrant mountains. But as the concept of environmental protection became more recognized, woodcutters gradually changed to forest rangers, and bird catchers changed to bird rangers. As the most beloved mascot of Yunnan, Asian elephants received the most protection. Poaching and illegal trade were punished severely, which formed an effective deterrent and basically eliminated the poaching of Asian elephants in Yunnan.

Second and more importantly is to strengthen the construction, protection, and restoration of Asian elephant habitats. In recent years, Yunnan Province has built eleven nature reserves in the main distribution areas of Asian elephants, with a total area of 5,098 square kilometers.

The pilot project of habitat restoration and reconstruction began in 2001, and an Implementation Plan for Habitat Protection and Restoration of Asian Elephants was prepared in 2019. By 2020, six square kilometers of habitat area were repaired. In Yunnan, people do not seek development at the expense of the living environment of wild animals because it is only meaningful when all living organisms develop together in peace.

Third, it is worth mentioning that scientific research on Asian elephants has been continuously carried out in Yunnan. Organizations and institutions such as the Asian Elephant Expert Committee, the Asian Elephant Research Center, and the Field Scientific Observation and Research Station of the Ministry of Education of the Yunnan Asian Elephant have been specially established. In 2018, Yunnan Province completed the Background Survey of Wild Asian Elephant Resources in Yunnan, China, which enabled comprehensive knowledge of the population, distribution, and activity tracking of the Asian elephants and individual recognition in common herds. These institutions played an important role in the trip of the Short Trunks. Their long-term accumulated knowledge and research practices made it possible to scientifically arrange the migration of elephants and protect the people and elephants on the way.

At the same time, Yunnan has formed a unique model in adopting and rescuing Asian elephants. With the establishment of Xishuangbanna Asian Elephant Breeding and Rescue Center in 2008, the field rescue team has participated in twenty rescue operations and successfully saved nineteen wild Asian elephants that have lost their self-care ability.

Among the Local Standards for Wildlife Protection in Yunnan Province issued in 2021, three were for Asian elephants. The Technical Regulations for the Field Rescue of Asian Elephants standardizes the workflow and requirements of field rescue from two aspects: management organization and rescue technology. The Technical Regulations for the Wild Population Monitoring of Asian Elephants specified the monitoring objects, contents, and indicators, and put forward reasonable procedures and technical methods for scientific monitoring in the future. In view of the key problems such as long pregnancies and difficult parental rearing of Asian elephants, the Technical Specifications for Artificially-Assisted Rearing of Asian Elephants put forward a set of scientific methods that can be used for reference.

For the sake of human and elephant safety, Yunnan has built a monitoring and emergency response system. The province has employed more than 100 full-time Asian elephant monitors to work under a "two-in-one" monitoring system, and a monitoring and early warning center was also established in Xishuangbanna. In 2017, it began to apply an integrated means of manual tracking, fixed-point equipment, and UAVs to monitor the distribution, quantity, and activities of Asian elephants in real-time. It also broadcast the activities of Asian elephants to the residents in the distribution area through a customized app so that people could avoid the elephants in time. Right now, there is an Emergency Plan for the Protection and Security of Asian Elephants for every distribution area, which reduces the probability of human-elephant encounters. Villages have been relocated in many nature reserves. Fences and solar-powered elephant alert lights have also been installed along with strengthened constructions and facilities to create a safe living environment for the people.

Of course, Asian elephants are not unique to China, and those in China often "travel abroad." To ensure their safety, Yunnan promoted the cross-border joint protection between China and Laos. For example, the cooperation agreement between Yunnan Xishuangbanna National Nature Reserve Administration and the three northern provinces of Laos helped to materialize five joint protection areas with a total length of about 220 kilometers and an area of about 2,000 square kilometers, starting from "Shangyong China–Nam Ha Laos" in the south to "Mengla China–Phongsali Laos" in the north.

What Does the Home of Elephants Look Like?

What the Short Trunks saw during their journey was beautiful, but the views of their homeland are equally fine. Among the many "tips" on elephant protection, habitat construction is considered the most effective. Let's now take a closer look at the home of the elephants.

For years, Yunnan has taken various measures to build an ideal home for Asian elephants. Several nature reserves on the prefecture- and county-level have been established in Xishuangbanna, making the actual space of the nature reserve from 2,667 square kilometers to 4,152 square kilometers. Pu'er City plans to build a 6.7-square-kilometer food source base to provide important supplies for Asian elephants in the food shortage season. In addition, Xishuangbanna has also restored more than 5.3 square kilometers of habitat and food source to plant tiger grass, banana, bamboo, and other plants favored by Asian elephants.

Xishuangbanna National Nature Reserve in Yunnan Province is the main habitat for Asian elephants before the species spread. There it protects the forest ecosystem of a tropical rainforest, a seasonal forest, and a monsoon evergreen broad-leaved forest, as well as rare wild animals and plants such as the Asian elephant and Parashorea chinensis (a tall, endangered evergreen tree).

The habitat outside the nature reserve also maintains high forest coverage. By the end of 2020, the forest coverage rate of Xishuangbanna Prefecture was 81.34%. It has a forest area of 15,550 square kilometers including 9,700 square kilometers of natural forest. The forest coverage rate of Pu'er City was 74.59%. It has a forest area of 33,030 square kilometers including 23,920 square kilometers of natural forest.

Xishuangbanna Prefecture has continuously strengthened the construction and management of wildlife habitats dominated by nature reserves. It has vigorously restored the tropical rainforest ecosystem by means of natural restoration and artificial restoration, prepared the construction plan of the Asian elephant protection project, promoted the construction of the Asian elephant protection and control areas, and continuously repaired the habitats of wild animals such as Asian elephants. Gradually, the goals of "human-elephant isolation" and "human-elephant harmony" were achieved.

Pu'er City is also increasing investment in biodiversity protection. It has implemented a number of projects, such as the protection of rare and endangered animals and plants, the construction of national wetland parks, the control of soil and water loss in key areas, and the building of more than 2.6 square kilometers of Asian elephant food source base.

The Nangunhe National Nature Reserve in Lincang aims to protect the tropical rainforest ecological environment and endangered animals such as wild Asian elephants, Indochinese tigers, and the white-handed gibbons. The forest coverage of this reserve is 93.4%. In recent years, the Administration and Protection Bureau of this reserve has taken a number of measures to promote biodiversity protection, such as consolidating the foundation of resource protection and simultaneously promoting management and scientific research.

The Whereabouts of the Elephants Is Well Known

The early warning and monitoring of elephants, according to experts, is the top priority of Asian elephant protection.

To timely observe the activities of Asian elephants, several villagers who are familiar with the local environment are appointed early warning and monitoring personnel of Asian elephants in Naji Village, Simao District, Pu'er City. Every morning, before farmers go out to work, the monitors will release early warning information through SMS or Wechat platform so that the masses can accurately receive the movement tracks of elephants and avoid them in time.

After years of exploration, Xishuangbanna Prefecture has established a diversified monitoring and early warning system with monitoring personnel and UAV tracking. The Scientific Research Institute of the reserve has now basically mastered the distribution of wild Asian elephants. In November 2019, with the support of national project construction, 605 infrared cameras and 21 cameras were deployed in and around the reserve. Together with the technologies of Artificial Intelligence, Cloud Computing, and the Internet of Things, they formed a comprehensive Asian elephant monitoring and early warning protection system. For the densely populated areas frequently visited by elephants, physical isolation was also adopted to separate human and elephant activities and avoid head-on conflicts.

More new technologies such as Beidou high-precision location service and short message communication service will be introduced to the local departments' elephant protection projects in order to better grasp the dynamics of the herds. Relevant tests are already in progress.

In 2018, Xishuangbanna Prefecture built the first Asian elephant monitoring and early warning center in China; in November 2019, Xishuangbanna Prefecture built an Asian elephant monitoring and early warning protection system, and continued to use scientific and technological innovation to improve the monitoring and early warning ability; in January 2021, Pu'er City built the first

Asian elephant monitoring tower in China to strengthen the monitoring and early warning efficiency.

Of course, strict monitoring is to avoid human-elephant conflicts and strengthen the protection of wild Asian elephants. These technologies will hardly affect the lives of Asian elephants. In the following section, more of Yunnan's elephant protection experiences and practices will be introduced.

Province-Level Headquarters of Safety Prevention and Emergency Response for Yunnan Northward Migrating Elephant Herd

On May 27, 2021, when the Short Trunks entered Eshan County in Yuxi, Yunnan Province quickly formed a provincial headquarters of safety prevention and emergency response for the northward moving herd. It carried out 24-hour tracking and monitoring and "went north side by side" with the elephants for the safety of the residents and elephants.

There has never been such an organization before. Every morning, the on-site headquarters would hold a dispatching meeting for nine working groups: the comprehensive coordination group, monitoring and early warning group, feeding guidance group, safety prevention group, relocation assistance working group, on-site control group, publicity working group, loss compensation group, and comprehensive support group. Personnel from the provincial and local departments of forestry, emergency services, public security, forest fire control, power, transportation, and others would all be present. Together, they would predict the next stop of the herd based on topographical conditions, channels, ground crops, and the elephants' daily habits.

Greatly impressed by such huge effort and dedication, CNN news reported: "In order to prevent any conflict between people and elephants, China has even established a 24-hour command center to monitor the whereabouts of elephants."

3

The "Bodyguards" of the Elephants

When the Short Trunks moved north, the monitoring team members of the Yunnan Provincial Forest Fire Brigade turned into "elephant chasers," professional "elephant photographers," and "elephant bodyguards." They have captured countless precious moments of the herd lying and sleeping together, the little elephants wrestling, trying on "straw hats," and practicing "martial arts" in the shade, all vividly telling the wonderful story in Yunnan to the world.

However, the work that each photo and video took to make was unimaginable. The monitoring members spent 24 hours "chasing elephants" every day for several hundred days in succession.

Some of them lost five kilograms in seven days because of the pressure; their sons complained "You are not my dad now, but 'the elephants' dad'"; some were even too busy to eat ...

The "Eyes" of the "Elephant Chaser Team"

The monitoring members have good eyes. All of them are good at long-distance observation and close-up observation whether through the naked eye, camera lens, or UAV screen. They could always find the elephants and explore as much information as possible from their daily activities, including current living conditions, possible moving directions, and interesting details.

The monitoring members are also the "eyes" of the whole "elephant chaser team." They need to send the monitoring pictures back to the joint headquarters in real-time so as to provide a reference basis for studying the dynamics of the herd and making deployments in advance. Wherever the elephants went, the monitoring team followed. Of course, these "elephant chasers" never disturbed the elephants. They had strict demands for the flight altitude of the drones and the location of the photographers.

Thanks to their hard work, people can observe every move of wild Asian elephants in such a rich and concentrated way on the Net.

Staying Awake with the Elephants

Chasing elephants sounds like a romantic job, but it is actually extremely exhausting both physically and mentally.

Aside from eating and sleeping in the open air, the "elephant chasers" also needed to adapt to the elephants' body clocks.

The Short Trunks liked to wander in the forest during the day and travel in the evening. This meant that the "elephant chasers" were also forced to work at night. The challenge could be perceived.

Elephants have very unique and complicated personalities, and they often appeared to be capricious, self-centered, and elusive. This made it difficult even for the monitoring staff to predict their movement.

Therefore, the members were always on high alert in each monitoring action so as to not lose track of the wild elephants and prevent human-elephant conflicts.

The advent of the rainy season posed a greater challenge to the monitoring work. In a thunderstorm, the UAVs were at risk of being struck by lightning and water seepage when taking off. In addition, the mountains were often shrouded in fog after rain, making it difficult to accurately locate the herd even with infrared induction.

Therefore, when the UAVs and infrared telescopes did not work, the "elephant chasers" had to fully rely on manpower to find the elephants. They proceeded with heavy loads in the heavy rain. Every discovery—whether a footprint or a fecal trace—could make their day.

Those Unforgettable "First Times"

- THE FIRST TIME SEEING THE HERD SLEEPING TOGETHER

Narrator: Fu Cong, advocate of the wild Asian elephant search and monitoring team at the Yunnan Provincial Forest Fire Brigade:

When I saw the picture of elephants sleeping together for the first time, I found it interesting that they all slept facing the same direction and had their four legs curled up. It was so neat and so cute. There is another picture that I thought was very sweet: the herd always keeps the baby elephant in the middle while they sleep, and there is always an elephant on guard to protect the others. These showed the strict discipline and strong teamwork ability of these animals.

- THE FIRST TIME ENCOUNTERING THE HERD

Narrator: Shao Shan, driver of UAV group A of the search and monitoring team at the Yunnan Provincial Forest Fire Brigade:

My first encounter with the elephants was at the transfer in Hongta District, Yuxi City. They were only 30 meters away from us. It was my first time being so close to the herd, and I felt they were much bigger and taller than I thought. I was both curious and afraid. For safety, we held our breath, stalled the car, turned off the lights, and observed quietly. I kept wondering: what should we do if the elephants came toward us? We found our breath again after the elephants left, and then we had to quickly move to the next observation point.

• THE FIRST TIME CELEBRATING A HOLIDAY IN LOCAL VILLAGERS' HOME

Narrator: Duan Xianneng, member of UAV group C of the search and monitoring team at the Yunnan Provincial Forest Fire Brigade:

The traditional Dragon Boat Festival arrived during our mission. At that time, we were on a night-flight mission. All we wanted was not to lose the herd so that the local people could have a good festival. The kind local villagers brought us *zongzi* (a traditional Chinese festival food made of glutinous rice) that they planned to sell in the market. They said that seeing our young people was like seeing their own children and that they should take care of us like taking care of their own children. I am a recruit. I used to hear others say, "The army and the people are families." Now that I have experienced it myself, I understand this sentence better and feel the importance of my responsibility more deeply.

• THE FIRST TIME WORKING IN THE MEDIA SPOTLIGHT

Narrator: Duan Mengchao, leader of UAV group C of the search and monitoring team at the Yunnan Provincial Forest Fire Brigade:

I have never seen so much media before, and I never thought my work would be related to media. They have helped to publicize the work of our monitoring team members and make us popular "elephant chasers" on the Internet. But we are still focusing on monitoring the elephants, helping people, and cooperating with the joint command. The media reported the location of the elephant herd in time to let people take precautions in advance. This was also a kind of support for our work from the perspective of prevention and control.

These "elephant chasers" observed the elephants every day, and accompanied them to grow. In the autumn of 2021, when the Short Trunks returned home, the "elephant chasers" finally breathed a sigh of relief. However, after only a few days, they began to miss their old friends. When they saw the herd again from the monitoring pictures, the team members all smiled a happy, gratified smile to find that they have gained some weight.

Writing to My Future Self

Writer: Yang Xiangyu, group leader of the search and monitoring team at the Yunnan Provincial Forest Fire Brigade:

Dear Yang Xiangyu,

How are you?

You must remember meeting fifteen Asian elephants in the summer of 2021. What incredible fate! You have spent ninety-one days and nights watching out for them and traveled with them for more than 1,000 kilometers. What wonderful memories! How are they doing now? I guess they are living happily in the National Park, and maybe many more of them are

Yang Xiangyu, group leader of the search and monitoring team at the Yunnan Provincial Forest Fire Brigade.

strolling and enjoying their lives in the beautiful landscape of China. On this colorful planet, humans and Asian elephants live peacefully together. Wild animals no longer decrease in population, the deserts of yesterday have become oases, meadows and cities are covered with flowers and vegetation, and our children run freely under a clear blue sky ... The sky is so blue, the mountains so green—it must be the homeland that we all dream of living in!

Writer: Guan Yuhao, member of group B of the search and monitoring team at the Yunnan Provincial Forest Fire Brigade:

Taking off my olive-green fatigue, I put on a fiery-blue uniform.
I am a soldier, from the army to the local.
My blood is burning; my heart is beating,
I fight on the front line where I am needed.
My career is dangerous,
and it keeps my family in constant anxiety and concern.
But I am still crazily in love with it.
I am willing to give my life to it
because I am confident and determined to serve my country.
I often think if I chose firefighting or
did firefighting complete me.
The most important thing is
what I am protecting
as well as what my beliefs and missions are.
Looking forward,
I will protect the peaceful lives of my people,
always remembering my aspiration and destiny to serve.
I was a boy when I left home,
but I will be a man when I come back.
I will never regret putting on the color of the fiery blue.

The Story behind the Elephants' Popular Sleeping Photo

A picture of the sleeping elephants went viral with their magic journey. It was taken by one of the "elephant chasers" Zhang Xiong, leader of the emergency communication and vehicle service support department and leader of group A of the wild Asian elephant search and monitoring team at the Yunnan Provincial Forest Fire Brigade.

Zhang never expected the picture to become so famous. He said he was only recording an authentic scene of the elephants' nap time that made him feel warm and loving.

Zhang introduced that this photo was taken at about 10:30 a.m. on June 7, 2021, the time when the staff members changed shifts. "Before the shift, I need to clearly know the number and location of the elephants. When I operated the UAV to get above the elephants, the first I saw was the elephants sleeping in a specific pattern. They basically all had their trunks and legs curled up and facing the same direction."

Zhang Xiong said that he was both shocked and curious to see this. During the usual monitoring process, the staff members thought the elephants were naughty, but they didn't expect them to be so "disciplined" when they slept. "This picture blew my mind because we have monitored the elephants for so long but have never seen them asleep. This is such a valuable moment."

In addition to Zhang, there were many others "fighting in the front line" of monitoring the elephants. They had been chasing and protecting the elephants for more than ninety days and had taken many videos about them. They were referred to as "the most brilliant elephant chasers" on the Internet.

Their monitoring tasks helped them grow stronger. They believe that the task of wild Asian elephant search and monitoring is not to simply see where the elephant herd is but to constantly observe the distance between the elephant herd and the residents, to prevent human-elephant conflicts, to better protect the safety of everyone, and to record the elephants' activities for scientific purposes.

Zhang reflected on his more than two hundred times crossing mountains and rivers with the elephants. The elephants raised their trunks to "say hello" to the drones, the baby elephants "watered" the crops with the pipes, two young fellows picked up a fight while taking a bath, they sometimes interacted with dogs, chickens, and goats, and sometimes "stole" bananas, sugarcane, corn, and other crops from the villagers ... He remembered everything as clearly as if they had happened just yesterday.

Zhang is a first-class UAV technician, and he also knows a lot about wild Asian elephants. Whenever a new member joined in, they were sent to work under Zhang first. Today, he has trained more than twenty wild Asian elephant monitors for the team and the Kunming Aerial Survey Center.

"Elephants are our good friends. We live in the global village together." Zhang believes the northward migration of the elephants that has attracted much attention at home and abroad is a major event in the field of ecological civilization and biodiversity protection. As a forest firefighter, he feels the proudest and most honored to guard the safety of the people and the elephants as well as to present to the world a colorful Yunnan and a beautiful China.

4

A Haven for Asian Elephants

The Asian elephant is one of the flagship species in Yunnan, and the Yunnan people love them dearly. The construction of the National Nature Reserve has long been planned, and now the construction of Asian Elephant National Park is also actively proceeding.

Most Asian elephants, including the Short Trunks, live in Xishuangbanna National Nature Reserve in Yunnan Province. Founded in 1958, it is one of the first twenty nature reserves established in China with the largest and highly concentrated Asian elephant population.

It has five geographically unconnected sub-reserves: Mengyang, Menglun, Mengla, Shangyong, and Man'gao, with a total of 2,425 square kilometers. It was promoted to be a National Nature Reserve in 1986, and in 1993, it joined the UNESCO Man and Biosphere Program and became a haven for most Asian elephants in China.

Elephants, the Engineers of Tropical Rainforests

Yunnan Xishuangbanna National Nature Reserve is a large-scale comprehensive nature reserve with the main purpose of protecting the tropical forest ecosystem and rare wild animals and plants. It is the largest primitive tropical forest area in

China with relatively complete preservation of the tropical forest ecosystem and extremely rich biological resources.

Today, the forest coverage rate of the whole reserve has reached 97.02%, which is 10-15% higher than when the reserve was established in 1958. The habitat outside the nature reserve also maintains high forest coverage, and the natural forest accounts for the majority.

The lush environment and the mild, humid climate make the reserve an ideal home for Asian elephants.

They live in a "matriarchal clan" society. Family members are composed of female elephants and young male elephants, usually a female elephant with her children. Sometimes several families live together, like the Short Trunks we are familiar with.

In the documentary *Big & Little Tramps*, Guo Xianming, director of the Scientific Research Institute of the Xishuangbanna Nature Reserve in Yunnan, says that elephants are the "engineers of tropical rainforests."

The tunnels and paths that elephants open up with their huge bodies create open spaces and gaps in forests, which enable the sun to reach low plants such as herbs and shrubs and create conditions for the plant renewal of the whole rainforest. Their giant footprints create small puddles to facilitate the survival and reproduction of amphibians and insects. Asian elephants make excellent seed disseminators with their wide sphere of activities and long migration routes. Their large intake of plants will to some extent promote the latter's spread and regeneration, and their feces will also provide nutrients for the growth of fungi and seeds as well as a living and breeding place for beetles, termites, ants, and other small animals. In addition, Asian elephants dig caves in the rainforest with their trunks and tusks to feed on the soil to supplement salt and minerals, and the caves will provide shelters for other wild animals.

Basically, Asian elephants are protecting the biodiversity of the whole region like no others. Once their populations degenerate, there will be a huge negative impact not only on the species but also on their living ecosystem.

What Does the "Elephant Restaurant" Look Like?

Asian elephants eat a variety of plants and fruits. These champion eaters can consume more than 100 kilograms of food every day. In the forest gaps opened by the Asian elephants, the sun shines through the dense forest and all kinds of low herbs with delicate branches and leaves will grow in this open space for elephants and other animals to feed on.

However, with the strengthening of ecosystem protection and management, the tall and dense forest provides shelter for Asian elephants but fails to meet their dietary needs. To ensure the survival and reproduction of wild Asian elephants, the Reserve took the lead in putting forward the concept of the Asian Elephant Food Source Base along with the one square kilometer forest restoration.

Around 2010, the construction of the Wild Asian Elephant Food Source Base began in the Lianhuatang area in the Reserve by the Lancang River, far away from villages. Attempts have been made to repair the Food Source Base by artificially planting local plants the wild Asian elephants like (such as paper mulberry and tiger grass). This relatively flat area is surrounded by forests and has ponds nearby, which is very in line with the elephants' needs for habitat.

Through infrared cameras, we have seen many wild animals such as Asian elephant, Indian bison, sambar deer, and wild boar come to dine at the "elephant restaurant" in Lianhuatang.

There is another "elephant restaurant" at the Guanping grounds-keepers' station in Mengyang Sub-Reserve.

This gentle hillside was reclaimed by nearby villagers to grow corn and soybeans. When elephants started foraging around their habitats, they often invaded these cultivated lands. Today, these lands are used for growing bananas and tiger grass for the "elephant restaurant."

At present, with the joint efforts of the government and social institutions, the cumulative scale of Asian Elephant Food Source Bases in Xishuangbanna has reached about five square kilometers.

The number of wild Asian elephants in Jinghong City has increased from about 80 by the end of the twentieth century to about 185 today. Their activity range in Jinghong City has reached 3,500 square kilometers. In 2021, according to the activity track of Asian elephants, the "elephant restaurant" in the joint jurisdiction of Dadugang Township, Jingne Township, and Mengwang Township near the Reserve was also put into use. This "elephant restaurant" has a total investment of one million RMB. It has transformed and established 0.7 square kilometers for tiger grass (0.23 square kilometers) and a banana (0.22 square kilometers) plantation. There are also five nitrite ponds nearby. Salt was put in to meet the Asian elephants' physiological need for salt.

The Elephant Early Warning and Monitoring System

The population of wild Asian elephants is increasing year by year, and the Reserve has reached a relatively saturated state. With the reduction of food sources in the habitat, elephants may go out of the Reserve in autumn and winter trying to open up new habitats and searching for food. Once Asian elephants enter the human communities, they will have secured access to rich crops. After feeding on these crops for some time, their diet will gradually change, and their returning to the original habitat will also significantly decrease.

More than a thousand years ago, elephants had already begun to roam the villages and brought trouble to the villagers. The *History of the Song Dynasty* recorded: "In the third year of the Jianlong period (962 AD), elephants went to Huangpi County. They hid in the forests and ate the villagers' crops. Then they went to An, Fu, Xiang, and Tang Prefectures and invaded the farmers' fields." Wu Cui also described wild elephants entering the village in his *Notes upon Seeing and Hearing*: "My colleague Zheng Wenzhen is from Chaoyang. He says the elephants are of great harm to the local residents. Whenever they turned away from their vegetables and crops, the elephants will immediately invade the field and eat them all."

An adult Asian elephant weighs several tons. Its huge body has strong destructive power, and it needs a great amount of food every day. The villages where the elephants have visited are likely to face serious losses. Asian elephants have very good memories. They may return to places they have been to before.

The human-elephant conflict in this way has gradually become prominent.

To alleviate this conflict, we must first know the population of Asian elephants well.

Yunnan has hundreds of full-time Asian elephant monitors. Every morning, they go out to "look for" elephants and send early warning information by telephone, SMS, mobile apps and other means.

The first Asian elephant protection, monitoring, and early warning system in China was built in the Reserve to realize real-time monitoring, tracking, and protection of elephants through 5G, Internet of Things, Cloud Computing, big data, Artificial Intelligence, and other advanced technologies. Cameras capture the movements of elephants 24 hours a day. Any sign of movement will start the AI recognition system, which will send out a broadcast to the villagers through phones and smart speakers if the alert comes from an Asian elephant.

Xiangyanjing Village is located on the edge of Mengyang Sub-Reserve and is where Asian elephants spend a lot of time. Local villagers still remember that due to elephants' frequent visits, they haven't harvested rice and corn for years. Elephants enter and pass through the village about forty times a year on average. They can break into houses for food, causing property losses and injuries to some villagers. Sometimes elephants even enter the village during the day, and the villagers dare not leave the children outdoors.

In 2017, a 1,350-meter-long elephant guardrail was built in Xiangyanjing Village, the first pilot village of Asian elephant guardrail in China. The villagers said, "Now elephants can't come in anymore. We can sleep better at night.

The Elephants' "Transnational Tour"

In the early morning of January 27, 2018, a wild Asian elephant came to the Chahe border checkpoint on the China–Laos border and "swaggered" across the border guard duty barrier. After a ninety-two-minute "transnational tour" to Laos, this elephant returned to China through the border inspection channel.

On the evenings of March 22 and 23, 2021, a slightly smaller elephant sneaked into the scenic spot in Xishuangbanna to see the Parashorea chinensis (a large evergreen tree). It leisurely toured around the scenic spot and feasted on the bananas.

The free "transnational tours" of these two elephants proved the positive results of cross-border ecological protection of wild Asian elephants in Yunnan.

In the Xishuangbanna National Nature Reserve, the sub-reserves of Mengla and Shangyong share border lines with Laos for 108 kilometers. For them, no passport is needed for "traveling abroad."

Back in 2006, the former Xishuangbanna National Nature Reserve Administration has already put forward the concept of "cross-border joint protection of biodiversity between China and Laos" and established a mechanism with Nam Ha National Protected Area in Luang Namtha Province, Laos.

At the end of 2009, China and Laos officially demarcated the first China–Laos cross-border joint protection area—"China Xishuangbanna Shangyong–Laos Lyang Namtha Nam Ha Laos biodiversity joint protection area."

In December 2012, the Reserve signed an agreement with the three northern provinces of Laos to build a 220-kilometer-long, 2,000-square-kilometer "China–Laos border joint protection area" that is also a green ecological corridor between the two countries.

Right now, the exchange and cooperation between the two countries in the China-Laos joint cross-border biodiversity protection and exchange mechanism has risen from the department level to the government level. The establishment of joint protection areas has driven and guided neighboring countries to actively participate in biodiversity protection. It has helped expanding cooperation with Southeast Asian neighboring countries, promoting the biodiversity protection model at the front line of Yunnan Province, strengthening the construction of border ecological security barriers, and creating a new way for the region to build a community of life.

Artificial Nitrite Ponds

In order to help the elephants acquire salt and minerals, the Reserve set up artificial nitrite ponds in the forests or near the food source bases. In 2017, the Administration and Protection Bureau of the Xishuangbanna Reserve selected a natural nitrite pond with dense surrounding primitive forests in Mengyang Sub-Reserve and expanded it into a 25 square meters' artificial nitrite pond. Because the nitrite pond is located in the permeable zone and the soil contains a lot of salt, it forms a natural salty pond that can meet the needs of all wild animals.

In 2018, the infrared cameras captured groups of Asian elephants, muntjacs, wild boars, and macaques coming to the nitrite pond. Two brownish muntjacs with white spots came. They took turns to drink and watch for danger. Thirty or so macaques came. They played, drank, and enjoyed a sunbath. Even wild boars that hardly ever appear in groups came ... Together, they formed a harmonious scene of forest gathering.

5

Elephant Hospital and Birthing Room

It was a mysterious night talk.

March 6, 2021. Midnight. The air was moist and cool.

A strange visitor quietly came upon the Asian Elephant Breeding and Rescue Center in Xishuangbanna Dai Autonomous Prefecture, Yunnan Province.

It was a wild Asian elephant. No one knew about his arrival until seeing the video record.

At first, people thought he came to the Center for a midnight snack. He ate sixty or seventy sugarcanes and turned specifically to the Napier grass. Satisfied, he then laid down and napped for about forty-five minutes.

Just then, the real purpose of his visit was revealed. He went straight to the "elephant dorms" and began to "talk" to Yanyan, an elephant living in the Center.

No one knew what they said. But their conversation lasted the whole night.

At dawn, the sky brightened on the East. The strange elephant left and disappeared into the wilderness, as quickly and quietly as when it came.

If Asian elephants can write their histories like humans, this mysterious night talk will certainly be included.

Maybe, it was a meeting between two old friends. After Yanyan lived in the Breeding and Rescue Center, he lost contact with his friend.

Fearing that Yanyan might be in danger, his friend looked everywhere for him. Finally, he found the Breeding and Rescue Center.

So, in the dark night, he carried out his plan. He first pretended to be a "glutton" who came to dine in the dark, then he took a nap to cover his act.

At last, he saw Yanyan, but things were different from what he imagined ... Yanyan was doing very well.

Later, the two friends shared their stories. Yanyan's friend changed his mind and gave up on his "rescue" plan. He was not worried about Yanyan in the Center anymore.

Cure the Pain from the Past

If Asian elephants can write diaries or logs like us, it is very likely that they will mention the Asian Elephants Breeding and Rescue Center.

Not only because this is where the "mysterious night talk" took place but also because of its importance to the wild Asian elephants.

Adjacent to the Wild Elephant Valley, it is the only research base in China that centers on Asian elephant rescue and breeding.

As one of the Six Major National Forestry Projects (National Wildlife Protection and Natural Reserve Construction Project), the "Fifteen Species Rescue Plan" implemented in Yunnan, the Asian Elephant Breeding and Rescue Center has been committed to the receiving, rescuing, breeding, and treating Asian elephants since it was put into use in 2008. It aims to protect and save the wild Asian elephants in China, protect biodiversity, and maintain natural ecological balance.

Of course, in a place where Asian elephants are so concentrated, protection is always a long-standing project.

In 2005, people found a three-year-old baby elephant in the river channel under the Wild Elephant Valley observatory. Her left hind leg was injured by a steel trap, and the wound was badly infected and festering. The Forestry Department, the Nature Reserve Management Bureau, and the Wild Elephant Valley Scenic

Spot Office immediately set up a rescue team of eighty-one people to rescue the baby elephant.

They anesthetized the baby elephant and transferred her to safety. There, they took off the trap from her leg and provided emergency treatment to the wound.

Frightened and alerted, the baby elephant did not cooperate with the treatment. One day, she broke free from the chain and ran away when she heard the call of her family. When they found out about this, the staff members at the Center were extremely worried that the wild environment would lead to the deterioration of her injury.

When the staff found the baby elephant, the muscles on her injured leg had given off a stench, and they could see bones through the wound. They thus transferred the baby elephant to Mengyang for treatment so that she could recover as soon as possible. Six months later, the baby elephant's wound gradually healed.

This was the famous Ranran, the first successfully rescued wild elephant in China.

Her name (which uses 然 rán, the second Chinese character in the word for "nature" 自然 zìrán) was to remember that nature was where she was rescued, and it also conveys people's wishes for her to return to nature and return home early.

Aside from Ranran, there was also the little homeless Xiaoqiang, who was seriously malnourished when he was found at ten months old; Yangniu, who was abandoned by her mother when she was less than one week old, suffering from a serious umbilical infection and frequently went into a coma when found; Pingping, whose hip was badly infected and inflamed from injury; Kunliu, who fell off a steep eighty-meter-high hill during a fight with other male elephants ... Over the years, the Center has already rescued more than twenty wild Asian elephants.

Today, nine wild Asian elephants that have lost their ability to survive in the wild are still receiving treatment and rehabilitation training in the Center. They are well taken care of, but they are also preparing to return to nature when they are ready.

Light up the Future

In addition to rescuing, breeding is also an important responsibility of the Center.

In 2017, a baby elephant was born here. It was the first Asian elephant in Yunnan bred with artificial assistance. Its birth marked a new breakthrough in China's Asian elephant breeding technology.

In 2020, the female elephant Pingzai successfully gave birth to her baby daughter, who was also her third calf. To date, the Asian Elephant Breeding and Rescue Center has successfully bred nine baby elephants and has successfully assisted in the breeding of four of them. These were valuable empirical experiences that the Center has accumulated in the breeding and artificial maintenance of Asian elephants.

Reproduction is not easy for Asian elephants. Their pregnancy rate through natural mating is low. Their pregnancy cycle is as long as 18–22 months, the lactation period is also more than two years, and each female elephant can only conceive one baby elephant at a time. In order to better protect the Asian elephants, the Center has made unremitting efforts to study artificially assisted breeding.

Since 2015, the Center has been testing the hormone levels of the female elephant Weilai. A suitable male elephant was then chosen at the best time as her mate, and, when the two had built an emotional bond, they were provided with a comfortable mating place. After Weilai was pregnant, the Center made a special recipe for her nutritional needs. This was the Center's first time to artificially assist elephant breeding, and the delivery and breeding were basically completed by the mother elephant. When the ninth baby elephant Jiumei was born, the whole pregnancy of the mother elephant was taken care of by very experienced staff members, and the calf was successfully delivered in time.

After years of research and practice, the Center has basically mastered the breeding and rearing behaviors of Asian elephants, and it has developed its own way of assisting the whole breeding process from conception to production. So far, it has achieved and maintained a 100% survival rate of baby elephants bred in the Center. One of them learned to stand only five minutes after it was born, which was the fastest among all newborn elephants in the country ever recorded.

A Thousand Times for You

Every day from 8 a.m. to 5 p.m., the Asian elephants in the Breeding and Rescue Center will go to the nearby forest for adaptive survival training accompanied by "elephant dads," the nursing staff members at the Center who take care of the elephants day and night.

"We can't let them lose their ability to survive in the wild because of our help," said Xiong Chaoyong, the "elephant dad" of Ranran. When Ranran was rescued, Xiong, who had experience in elephant care, offered to take care of her. He taught Ranran to eat fruit and even moved his bed next to Ranran to look after her 24 hours a day. Slowly, Ranran began to trust humans. She received her treatment and her injury gradually healed. Before Xiong was married, he always joked that Ranran was his daughter. When he had his own child, he said Ranran was still his eldest daughter. In 2019, Ranran gave birth to her own daughter Xiaoqi, and Xiong became an "elephant grandpa."

In addition to the "elephant dads," the Breeding and Rescue Center also has "elephant doctors." Bao Mingwei's story as an "elephant doctor" also began with Ranran. At first, Ranran was highly alert and would not let people approach her. Bao could only put the medicine in a high-pressure sprayer and spray it on her wound. Later, Bao summarized a set of indicators suitable for wild elephants according to Ranran's data in different states. As the number of wild Asian elephants rescued by the Center increases, Bao invented a tranquilizer pipe blower that can anesthetize elephants from twenty meters away with a 100% success rate. It conquered the challenge of anesthetizing elephants at close range during field rescues.

Of course, at the Asian Elephant Breeding and Rescue Center all encounters will eventually lead to separation. The ultimate goal of all rescue and breeding methods is to help elephants safely return to nature and survive on their own. Their work is ongoing.

Apparently, after a long night talk, the strange visitor who we saw at the beginning of this chapter left relieved and assured that his friend Yanyan was doing well at the Breeding and Rescue Center.

He realized that Yanyan was not "missing," but was living a better life in the "hospitals," "birthing rooms," "dorms," and "restaurants" that humans built for them.

These people proved with their actions that human beings are willing to share their wisdom and experience in protecting this blue planet with elephants, their long-term neighbors, friends, and companions.

6

The "Elephant Dads" in Yunnan

The "elephant dads" in the Breeding and Rescue Center live with the elephants day and night and take care of them in all ways. They have rich experience in wild elephant rescuing and artificial breeding.

In April 2021, we met Chen Jiming, who was one of the more than twenty "elephant dads" in the Center. He was the first "elephant dad" of the five-year-old Yangniu, who had grown from a tiny little thing not as tall as a man's waist to a big girl weighing 1.3 tons and 1.7 meters tall.

"She only walks when I walk, and she stops when I stop ..." said Chen lovingly with a smile.

Yangniu is a very famous Asian elephant. On August 17, 2015, several elephants broke into a village in Simao District, Pu'er City and left behind a weak, injured newborn less than a month old.

The Center immediately took the baby elephant back, but there was no elephant milk for her. The researchers thus found three female goats to feed the baby elephant. Soon after, the baby elephant recovered, and people called her Yangniu, the "goat girl."

Now, Yangniu is already five years old. "She is very active, and she likes humans very much," said Yangniu's second "elephant dads" Li Tao and Wang Bo. They are taking over the responsibility of taking care of Yangniu from their teacher Chen Jiming. But whenever Chen is present, Yangniu only listens to him. No one can call her away from him.

Yangniu's affection for Chen derives from his meticulous care for her. In the summer of 2015, Chen was celebrating his son's birthday at home. When he was suddenly informed to take care of Yangniu, he immediately canceled his vacation and returned to the Center.

"I have wiped her and changed her diapers, but I never did that for my son." Over the past five years, Chen Jiming, who lives just next to Jinghong City, spent very little time at home. "In 2019, I spent about 350 days in the Center." Chen patted Yangniu and said.

When he first started interacting with Asian elephants, Chen was also very worried. "They are so big and so heavy. It's quite scary." But with the deepening of his work, he has already become part of the lives of the Asian elephants. "We live together on the Earth, so we should respect each other. This is very important for protecting and developing the world's biodiversity." said Chen.

To him, Asian elephants are intelligent animals with souls. After years of living together, he found their affection for each other has crossed the boundary between species. "Although they don't speak, I can see that they feel our kindness through their movement and voices."

During the interview, Chen had a race with Yangniu. He slowed down on purpose to let Yangniu win. The latter screamed loudly. "Do you hear that? That is Yangniu saying she's happy! The elephants in the Center are very healthy and very happy with their 'elephant dads.' I think the elephants in our country are the happiest elephants in the world!" Despite all the challenges in the elephant rescue work, everyone hopes these elephants could grow up, recover their health, and return to nature as soon as possible.

In the Center, Asian elephants frequently exercise in the primitive forest as part of their recovery training. The "elephant dads" go on excursions with the elephants almost every day. "We bring some glutinous rice or dry food with us when we go on these hikes. We set off in the morning and return at night." Chen and his colleagues rank at the top on the Center's "sport leaderboard" almost every day.

Today, there are twenty-six "elephant dads" in the Center. As the Center grows bigger, it brings up more gratified personnel for wild elephant rescuing and artificial breeding. Twenty-six-year-old Zhou Fangyi from Shandong has been in the Center for a year now. This young animal lover chose to stay in the Center for the elephants after doing his internship there during his graduate study.

Thanks to the efforts of "elephant dads" like Chen Jiming and Zhou Fangyi, new progress and breakthroughs have been made in Asian elephant breeding and rescuing, which has not only achieved good social and ecological benefits but also made positive contributions to the protection of Asian elephants and the construction of an ecological civilization.

7

Love and Prevention in Elementary School

Naji Elementary School in Yixiang Township, Simao District, Pu'er City, Yunnan Province, is also known as the "elephant-proof elementary school" because of its elephant fences and elephant prevention drills.

Here, children's lives are different because of the arrival of elephants. What interesting stories happened between them?

The Spiritual Elephants That Broke into School

"Naji" means "welcoming the propitious." In 2017 and 2019, Naji Elementary School welcomed some propitious guests twice. How did it happen?

It all started with an elephant from Xishuangbanna.

Chinese Asian elephants used to live in Xishuangbanna all year round. However, one day back in 1992, a "restless" lone elephant "secretly" planned to move. It went all the way north into the city of Pu'er.

Under its leadership, new elephant herds have been kept coming from Xishuangbanna to Pu'er to seize the new territory. They did not want to miss their share in this "cake cutting competition."

Because the ecological environment of Pu'er is improving, more and more elephants began to settle down in this city. So far, up to 181 elephants have been detected being active in the city on one day, which is more than half of all Asian elephants in China.

There are forty playful and curious elephants living in the forest near Naji Elementary School. They have visited the school twice. Fortunately, no one was hurt.

Their first visit was in 2017. Three elephants broke into the campus and made a complete mess. More than twenty palm trees with diameters of a bowl were uprooted and thrown all over the campus. The elephants ate up all the young leaves on them before they left.

In 2019, some of them returned. They broke into the school and began to ruin the facilities and trees there.

The witness of both events, the security guard of Naji Elementary School Tao Zhaobing still felt afraid in retrospect: "Thank goodness it was during the summer vacation; otherwise, I really don't know what could have happened!"

At that time, "How should people and elephants coexist?" and "What should we do if elephants break into the campus?" had become hot topics in the local area. Under this context, the "elephant-proof elementary school" came into being.

Learn to Live in Peace with the Elephants

To avoid human-elephant conflicts, the Pu'er City quickly launched an emergency plan after wild elephants broke into Naji Elementary School for the second time. What did they do?

When we arrived at the "elephant-proof elementary school," the first things we saw were the black and yellow steel fences at the gate. These tight protective fences are about 24 meters long and 3.2 meters high. They are built with 15 tons of steel. The elephants haven't come on campus since the fences were installed. Occasionally, some curious baby elephants will come and kick on the guardrail, but eventually they all give up upon confronting the obstacles.

If you walk into the campus, you will see that the several dozens of palm trees that once grew there are gone. Camphor trees and African tulip trees have been planted instead.

Palm trees are elephants' favorite plants. In order to prevent these "foodies" from coming for snacks again, the school has changed the plants into something that elephants don't like.

Additionally, the school also regularly carries out elephant prevention drills. When students are playing on the outdoor courts, they sometimes hear the sound of elephants played on the school's loudspeakers for the elephant prevention drills. When they hear this, the students will immediately run to the nearest school building in order to avoid the elephants.

It is worth mentioning that wildlife protection courses are compulsory in the "elephant-proof elementary school." These fun and informative lessons teach children how to live in harmony with elephants and treat their arrival scientifically.

Teacher: "Raise your hand if you saw the elephants! Can we go near the elephants and watch them when we see them?"

Students: "No!"

Teacher: "As we always say, what should we students do when we see elephants on campus? How should we protect ourselves on our ways to and from school?"

Students: "Keep away from them."

This is a live scene in the wildlife protection course of the "elephant-proof elementary school" and also a vivid practice of exploring the harmonious coexistence of humans and elephants. These lessons that center on the "harmonious coexistence between humans and nature" are worthy of promotion because protecting wild animals and the beauty of biodiversity is the mission and responsibility that each of us should shoulder.

At the same time, the "elephant-proof elementary school" has also actively explored faster, more effective, and more timely measures in elephant prevention. For example, all teachers and parents have joined the "wild elephant monitoring" Wechat group in the village. Whenever wild elephants appear near the school, the teachers and parents can quickly update and exchange information in the group at all times.

Zhu Hui who lives in Naji Village is an eleven-year-old student at the "elephant-proof elementary school." Her father accompanies her to and from school every day. She has seen elephants in the mountains from her classroom and in the farmland from the roof of her house.

In the years of living in peace with the elephants, the little girl reflects: "The elephants won't hurt us if we don't hurt them."

Today, elephants have become a scenic spot in the Naji Elementary School and in Naji Village. The name of the town where Naji Village is located has also changed from "Yexiang" (wild elephants) to "Yixiang" (embracing elephants). This gentle and cordial name coins the essence of "harmonious coexistence between humans and elephants."

A Letter to the Elephants

Dear elephant friends,

How are you?

Our little village was bathing in mist this morning when I woke up. I heard birds chirping from time to time, but something seemed missing. Suddenly, a huge figure came to me in a flashback. I asked my father, "I haven't heard elephants for a long time. Do you know where they have been?"

Father replied, "They have gone to the north. They are probably tired of staying here and want to see what the big cities look like." I felt lost when I heard this. Why did you choose to travel north?

For so many years, we have been familiar with your voices and used to the life with you nearby. Although you sometimes "steal" from the fields or cause mischief, we don't suffer too much losses and the government will always pay us back. But you are already part of our village now. You made our school famous on CCTV, and everyone around the world knows about us.

We have vast forests and your favorite bananas, corn, and rice. I know all your names. I hear that COP15 is being held in Kunming right now. Did you go to the conference to tell the world about our Naji Village in Pu'er? Or did you just decide to go on an impromptu trip?

My elephant friends, if you get tired from the journey, please come back! Everyone here, my family, my friends, and I miss you so much. I am worried that you would get lost, that you can't find good food away from home, and that you might get hurt.

Please come back home!

Cai Faxuan
Naji Elementary School

Xiaopuxi Village

Xiaopuxi Village at Jinuoshan Township, Jinghong City, Xishuangbanna Prefecture is a Jinuo village with only fifteen families in an uncultivated natural environment and of unique ethnic culture. In 2020, local villagers heard the cries of wild elephants. Later, the staff of Menglun Management and Protection Institute confirmed through UAV cameras and infrared image captures that there were eighteen elephants in the herd, with eleven adults and seven babies. This is also the second time that wild Asian elephants were discovered in Menglun Sub-Reserve after forty-one years. The improvement of the ecological environment has created conditions for the return of wild Asian elephants.

The harmonious coexistence of humans and elephants in Xiaopuxi Village has attracted the attention of environmental protectors and artists. Eight well-known original illustrated book authors have visited Xiaopuxi Village, sponsored by the public welfare activity "childlike innocence, nature, and welfare action, awaken the light of the Jinuo people." After a lot of in-depth exploration of the village and its surrounding environment, they carried out a public welfare wall painting project around the four themes of wild elephants, rainforests, insects, and machete cloth (a special cloth woven by the Jinuo people). In the future, Xiaopuxi Village is also expected to build a smart ecological bookstore, a rainforest bookstore, and an elephant nature school.

CHAPTER 3

All Approach the One Who Holds the *Dao*

"If we humans do not fail nature, nature will not fail us. Ecological civilization represents the development trend of human civilization. Let us join hands, follow the philosophy of ecological civilization and shoulder our responsibility for future generations. Let us make joint efforts to build a community of all life on Earth, and a clean and beautiful world for us all."

—On the afternoon of October 12, 2021, President Xi Jinping attended the leaders' summit of the 15th meeting of the Conference of the Parties to the Convention on Biological Diversity (COP15) held in Kunming via video link and delivered a keynote speech.

Guided by President Xi's idea of ecological civilization, China has been committed to protecting the ecological environment and biodiversity and attained prominent achievement. In Yunnan, in addition to a series of protection projects for Asian elephants, other species and nature reserves enjoy the benefits of environmental protection as well. A "Yunnan protection model" has come into place that vividly demonstrates a harmonious China of all things to the world.

"All Approach the One who holds the *Dao*." This sentence from the ancient classic philosophical book *Daode Jing* means wherever there are virtue and truth, where people will desire to go. The Short Trunks certainly proved that to be correct. The forest paths, the village roads, and the city streets ... the harmonious beauty of all things on Earth was everywhere they passed by.

1

"Model" Elephants

A small, delicate flower called *Ottelia acuminata*, with white petals and yellow pistils, grows in the famous Erhai Lake. It only grows where the water is clean and is thus viewed as an indicator of water quality.

There was a time when Erhai Lake was badly polluted and the *Ottelia acuminata* disappeared. But in recent years, as people started to take serious measures in protecting the picturesque Cang Mountain and the melodious Erhai Lake, the *Ottelia acuminata* has again blossomed on the water.

Both the *Ottelia acuminata* and the Asian elephants are barometers of the local ecosystem. As we can see from the Short Trunks' journey to the north, elephants are very fastidious about food and habitat. We can hardly imagine them living in a deserted, barren place. Elephants are decreasing all over the world now and have become an endangered species. In this light, it is gratifying that elephants have since ancient times always existed in China. It is true that their overall population is a lot smaller than before, but in recent years, we are seeing continuous growth in Yunnan, which is undoubtedly the result of excellent ecological protection brought to life by the traveling elephants.

Netizens around the world are fascinated by the Chinese people's high level of awareness of environmental protection. Not only were the elephants not hurt, but they were also treated with care. Before the story of the Short Trunks caused a sensation, news related to elephants was often upsetting. Most people have only seen "fragments" of them—heads, broken limbs, or pairs of blood-stained tusks.

In many parts of the world, poachers are pointing their guns at elephants, driven by the high demand for ivory. In order to call more attention to the increasingly worsened living conditions for Asian elephants and African elephants, the United Nations established World Elephant Day on August 12, 2012. People have tried various methods to arouse empathy and resonance to a wider public by shooting documentaries, making public service advertisements and revealing shocking pictures, etc., but these are still not enough to create a universal loving atmosphere for elephants.

Then the elephants came up with a solution. Everything seems easier after a pleasant, relaxing trip. Seeing the lovely pictures of the Short Trunks roaming, eating, and taking care of their calves, who would want to harm them and not let them enjoy a good journey?

Before we knew it, we were all "elephant guardians." As we watch the elephants, we learn more about their living habits and conditions, and we realize that these ancient friends are under serious survival risks.

While the Short Trunks and other wild elephants in Yunnan can receive attentive care, it is not true for all elephants in the world.

So, after we are amused and cured by the Short Trunks, we begin to think, "If only there were more stories like this!"

These "model" elephants have shown China's effective ecological protection in recent years and explained the real meaning of "harmony." At the same time, they also sent a warning to the world that ecological civilization is vital to the survival and development of life. In the face of environmental challenges, humans and animals are an integrated whole.

The Erhai Forum

On October 9, 2021, the 2021 Erhai Forum on Global Ecological Civilization Construction (hereinafter referred to as Erhai Forum) opened in Dali, Dali Bai

Autonomous Prefecture, Yunnan. As an important supporting activity of COP15, the forum brought together more than 300 Chinese and foreign representatives from the China International Communications Group (CICG), People's Government of Yunnan Province, China Public Relations Association (CPRA), Chinese Academy of Social Sciences (CASS), the Association of Southeast Asian Nations (ASEAN) Secretariat, and BRICs New Development Bank to seek the road of global ecological governance around the theme of "building an ecological civilization together for a beautiful planet."

In recent years, global environmental governance faces new difficulties and challenges. The concept of "lucid waters and lush mountains are invaluable assets" embodies the Chinese wisdom in constructing a global civilization and the profound thinking in developing human society and a clean, beautiful world. In Yunnan, the level of green development and the quality of ecological environment have continuously improved. The greener Cang Mountain and clearer Erhai Lake are epitomes of the remarkable achievements in biodiversity protection.

The forum pointed out that during the construction of a global ecological civilization, all parties need to focus on common concerns, convey rational voices, build exchange platforms, promote knowledge sharing, and advocate multilateralism and international cooperation for a better future for mankind.

Now, China's construction of ecological civilization has entered the fast lane. China has actively carried out international communication and shared its ideas, progress, and achievements in ecological construction. These are of great referential importance to global environmental governance and sustainable development and will inject vitality into global ecological civilization building.

2

Tips from the "Elephant Guardians" and "Elephant Parents"

Elephants are quiet. They have a loud voice, but they don't often speak. They live together as families, but they always seem to be alone compared with other animals that live in large groups. It's the loneliness that makes the long journey of the Short Trunks romantic—but is it really the case?

In fact, the Short Trunks are not lonely at all, and neither are the other wild Asian elephants in Yunnan.

Their human friends were with them throughout their journey. They either prepared food for the Short Trunks before they arrived at their next stop or guarded them quietly from a distance. More people supported the Short Trunks online, sending their love for these "model" elephants from all locations in the world.

After several hundred days of interactions, the elephants seem to have developed an emotional connection with people, said the "elephant chasers" of Yunnan Provincial Forest Fire Brigade. On their way back, the Short Trunks made the journey very easy for their "chasers" by deliberately following the route that people chose for them. They probably knew from the beginning that they were surrounded by kind, loving people. They expressed their gratitude by returning home "obediently" after they had enjoyed themselves.

Many people watched over the elephants on their way, and two of them are particularly worth mentioning: Chen Mingyong and Shen Qingzhong. Aside from making sure the magic journey of the Short Trunks went smoothly and peacefully, they also popularized all aspects of knowledge about wild Asian elephants in Yunnan to the world from a professional scientific point of view.

While the elephants' journey has come to an end, the merits of ecological protection will continue to last. From the research of Chen and Shen, we can see that the Short Trunks' northward movement was far more meaningful than a trip.

The Careful "Elephant Guardian"

Chen Mingyong is a professor at School of Ecology and Environment of Yunnan University and a leading expert on the safety prevention of the northward migrating Asian elephant herd. He followed the footprints of the Short Trunks for several months, paying close attention to their every move, raising reliable scientific countermeasures, and trying all means to guide the elephants back to their habitat in the south.

This was Chen's 36th year of studying animals after he majored in Wildlife Science in school, but the Short Trunks' journey still surprised him: it was the first time that Asian elephants in China moved north for such a long distance!

Chen Mingyong, the "elephant expert."

As a researcher, Chen worried about more things than regular "elephant watchers," such as the herd's destination or the climate, food, and water sources along the way.

Chen's worries were not without reason. After all, the further the elephants go north, the less suitable habitat they will find, and the easier it will be for human-elephant conflicts to happen. Chen was the most anxious about this. It was not until the Short Trunks safely returned to their habitat that he breathed a long sigh of relief. "The people and the elephants are all safe!" he always says with a proud smile.

Chen is an old friend of the elephants. After graduating in 1989, Chen entered the Research Institute of the Xishuangbanna National Nature Reserve Administration and put his knowledge into practice. In 2012, he began to teach and conduct research at Yunnan University. During his time in the Research Institute of Xishuangbanna Reserve, he carried out a great number of observations and research on Asian elephants and published many papers on the study of Asian elephants, Asian elephant protection corridor, folk knowledge, and cultural traditions of Asian elephant protection, and more.

Chen's responsibilities during the monitoring of the Short Trunks included observing and tracking the herd, participating in the prevention of human-elephant conflicts, and preparing and putting out food for the elephants.

Chen arrived at Mojiang County with his team as soon as the herd entered the public's vision. They used a lot of high-tech equipment such as infrared cameras, UAVs, and radio collars during the observation process. Infrared camera monitoring technology has been widely used in the investigation, monitoring, and research of wild animals because of its affordability, portability, and 24-hour uninterrupted data acquisition. For the huge and uninhibited Asian elephants, the UAV technology has greater advantages in long-distance monitoring and mobile tracking.

"A comprehensive monitoring and early warning system integrating Artificial Intelligence, Cloud Computing, Internet of Things, big data, and other technologies can weave the data collected by infrared cameras, video systems, UAVs, and other equipment into a large safety network. We can effectively prevent human-elephant conflicts by combining technological means and manual monitoring to timely release early warning information and take preventive measures." Chen said.

Chen sees the subtle emotions of elephants through their every movement. With the help of these high technologies, he has more clearly observed the elephants' timidity when crossing the highway, perceived the "communication" between the herd and an isolated elephant, experienced their panic when trying to cross the highway, and witnessed their ease and comfort when they have readapted to the environment after returning to the habitat. In order to closely track the whereabouts of the elephants, Chen and his colleagues have even stayed up for two days and nights.

The "Elephant Parent"

Chen Mingyong was not the only one taking care of the elephants' life and health. Shen Qingzhong, director of the Ecotourism Management Office of Xishuangbanna National Nature Reserve, has also been at the front-line headquarters keeping an eye on the elephants from the beginning of the close monitoring. He was present at every important turning point of the herd's journey.

Shen also has a long friendship with the elephants that has lasted for thirty years. This time, he was an "elephant parent" responsible for "clearing up" their waste. Every few days, Shen and his colleagues would collect and test the feces left by elephants for research. He explained that the responsibilities of "elephant parents"

Shen Qingzhong, the "elephant parent."

were to judge the elephants' health status, determine their food composition, and examine the genetic relationship among the herd members through fecal tests.

By checking the elephants' feces, Shen could know what the elephants ate the day before and whether they digested it well. He was relieved when he found that crude fiber, bark, and corn were all in the elephants' diet. "It's not easy for the elephants to cross different geographical, climatic, and ecological environments. Their strong adaptability provides a new reference for Asian elephant studies," he said.

As an on-site expert of the headquarters, Shen had a huge obligation. According to him, his work at the scene was actually "helping the elephant move back" with the fewest detours and human-elephant conflicts. He had to study the route of the herd every day, predict the herd's next movement according to the environment and road conditions ahead and give early warning information to the nearby villagers.

His predictions were highly reliable. Once, the elephants went to the mountains. Shen predicted that there was only one way suitable for these elephants not used to the bumpy mountain paths to take, and it turned out to be exactly as he expected.

This was not Shen's first "intimate contact" with the wild Asian elephants. The Breeding and Rescue Center at the Xishuangbanna National Nature Reserve in Yunnan where he worked has engaged in twenty-four rescue operations for Asian elephants since 2005.

Every rescue is an exploration that guides the direction for the next. The ultimate goal is to "rescue them and help them return to the wild."

Many of the rescued Asian elephants are juveniles. Unlike adult elephants, juvenile elephants are often weak and their physical condition tends to worsen after injury. At first, no one knew how to feed the baby elephants and how to take care of them to prevent aggravating the injury into becoming fatal. There were no special elephant veterinarians so the Center had to hire foreign experts for consultation. Shen realized that having professional "elephant doctors" was a must for rescuing wild Asian elephants.

In 2000, he recruited three graduates from the Yunnan Academy of Animal Husbandry and Veterinary at the Wild Elephant Valley scenic spot. Together, they accumulated and recorded their experience in rescue practices and shared them with forest rangers and monitors.

It has come to Shen's attention that elephants like to move around in open areas. They cannot be confined to a certain human-defined realm, nor can they live on the food provided by humans for a long time. Instead, they should be kept in the wild where they have access to a variety of plants to "get physical exercise in nature." The wild elephants' return to nature is a rigorous process that needs systematic evaluation. Shen has been working in this field for years focusing on scientific and reasonable planning for the wild elephants' return. Before reintroduction, the elephants must first receive long-term training in the wild, and they must also be monitored on their adaptation process to determine whether or not they can survive in nature. Only when the elephant is ready can the Center apply to a supervisory department for expert evaluation to judge whether it is competent enough to be released.

Shen said: "We still have a long way to go in rescuing wild elephants. Only when the reintegrated elephants have successfully started a new life and even reproduce can we say our rescue is really successful."

New Propositions in Elephant Protection

Chen Mingyong and Shen Qingzhong were invited to the News Center during the first phase of COP15. They attended the Cloud interview titled "Wild Asian Elephant's Travel: The Story of Asian Elephants' Northbound Immigration, Elephant Rescue, and the Elephants' Magic Trip with Forest Firefighters."

During the event, Chen and Shen brought up some new propositions on the subject of Asian elephant protection. They both mentioned the need to accelerate the construction of an Asian Elephant National Park, solve the problems of human-elephant conflicts and village development in the Asian elephant activity area, and establish the Asian elephant research center and field research base to better protect elephants.

According to Chen, researchers have gained a new understanding of the Asian elephant herd's activity and ability, the relationship among individual elephants, the relationship between elephants and humans, and so on. For example, it was previously believed that Asian elephants would not go to mountains above 1,300 meters, but the Short Trunks reached 2,200 meters above sea level and could walk freely on a 70-degree slope. Chen said, "We have gained new insights into the capabilities of Asian elephants."

"The distribution area of wild Asian elephants is expanding, and the population has recovered and increased. It indicates that Asian elephants have been well protected in Yunnan," said Shen. He raised the following suggestions: further improve the system at the management level, carry out necessary management and control of Asian elephants, and let elephants move in suitable areas; comprehensively analyze and summarize the lessons from the Short Trunks' northward migration and seek scientific confirmation; strengthen public education to further improve the public's awareness of protecting Asian elephants; provide education for villagers in the Asian elephant activity area to cooperate with relevant departments and form an elephant-loving, elephant-protecting, and elephant-avoiding atmosphere.

3

The Way to the World We Desire

Throughout their journey, the Short Trunks were personalized by the global netizens, and "cute" became their most eye-catching label.

When the huge beasts break into human "territory" and when their living space overlaps, human-elephant conflicts become a real obstacle in realizing "harmonious coexistence between humans and nature."

Where are the boundaries between humans and elephants? What is the key to harmonious coexistence? In the previous chapters, we learned about the relevant policies, system designs, insurance compensation, physical barriers, and other measures which come from the government and the public. Now, we will look at the exploration and research of a group of teachers and students on human-elephant coexistence.

Although it has been eighteen years since the story took place, the experience has deeply affected every participant until now. Today, they are ordinary people living in cities, but they harbor the greatest sincerity for nature. Maybe they do not have the power to change the world, but they are making contributions to our beautiful home through every action full of goodwill.

Like those people in the story, we are all looking for a way to the world we desire.

A Concern for the Destiny of Asian Elephants

Eighteen years ago, the Green Ecology Organization of Kunming No. 12 Middle School launched the 2003 international animal protection action week titled "Our Common Home: Protecting the Last Elephants on Earth" against the background of International Fund for Animal Welfare (IFAW)'s Animal Protection Week.

The event included lectures on "The Significance of the Yunnan Asian Elephant protection project" from protection experts, screening of the special publicity film *Our Common Home: Protecting the Last Elephants on Earth*, special programs of *Earth and Mankind and Resource Recovery* on the exploration channel, and a thematic discussion over "elephant living space and our future life." Many students cried when they saw the mutilated elephants in the videos. They developed an in-depth understanding of the environmental crisis and the threat of extinction that the elephants around us are now facing.

This event cultivated the idea of "starting from oneself" in protecting Asian elephants. With tears in their eyes, many students expressed their deep affection for the elephants as people's friends in the essay solicitation activity on the theme of "Man and Elephant" and wrote petitions calling for the prohibition of the ivory trade in class.

Although the international animal protection action week of Kunming No. 12 Middle School was only open to teachers and students in the school, the concern for biodiversity and ecological environment has triggered extensive discussions in many other schools in the city. Zheng Hua, a teacher from the extracurricular activities group of the High School Affiliated to Yunnan Normal University, was among many teachers who continued to pay attention to the event.

After multiple negotiations, an investigation team of thirteen students and five teachers from Kunming No. 12 Middle School and the High School Affiliated to Yunnan Normal University was formed. With a concern for the destiny of Asian elephants and the support of the IFAW, they went to several Asian elephant activity areas in Simao (today's Pu'er) in 2004 and carried out a biodiversity conservation investigation with the theme of "Caring for wild animals starts with caring for people." Their goal was to find possible solutions to the human-elephant conflicts in Simao and seek a more harmonious development model between man and nature.

A Vicious Cycle That Is Being Intercepted

Wild elephants have been living in the Simao area since ancient times. According to the *Simao County Annals*, the last three wild elephants around Caiyang River were killed by poachers in 1976. In the following sixteen years, the people in Simao never saw wild elephants due to environmental changes and human activity intensification. In fact, however, Simao is located at the edge of the Asian elephants' habitat and Asian elephants can enter Simao at any time.

Since their first return to Simao in 1992, wild elephants began to appear in Simao frequently. At the same time, the local announcement of closing mountains and banning hunting also provided a favorable ecological environment for the breeding and development of wild animals. But as the population of wild animals recovered, the cases of animals hurting people and ruining crops also increased. Over the past few years, wild elephants have injured people, damaged houses, and ruined crops in local communities, arousing panic and thus drawing the attention of the government and forestry departments. To prevent damage from the elephants, villagers often made noises, lit lights, set up fires, and dug protective ditches. These tactics against the invasion of wild Asian elephants only worked for a short time. Wild elephants soon got used to them because almost all the villages applied the same approaches.

The government and the people have been trying to find a good way to solve the problems with the farmlands and orchards ruined by the rare wild elephants protected by national laws. How should we better protect the wild Asian elephants while at the same time reducing the losses of local farmers?

The investigation team found a herd consisting of five females in Nanping County and Cuiyun Township in the middle of Simao. In the south, herds of one to more than a dozen elephants would occasionally enter Simao from Xishuangbanna.

The team's first investigation took place in Zhengwan Village, thirteen kilometers away from the city of Simao. In 1993, the villagers were excited to see the long-lost Asian elephants appear in groups. But as the elephants settled down in the mountains near the village, they began to frequently visit the farmland for food. It was a heavy blow to the villagers who took agricultural production as their main source of income. In addition, the elephants occasionally damaged houses and attacked humans, which aggravated the contradictions between people and elephants.

In 2000, the IFAW launched the "China Asian Elephant and Habitat Protection Project" in collaboration with the Forestry Department of Yunnan Province and the Simao government. The IFAW provided a "mutual aid fund," a small poverty alleviation loan to encourage the planting of alternative crops, reduce agricultural activities in the forest, and responded to the government's policy of returning farmland to forests to protect the habitat of Asian elephants.

The "mutual aid fund" group was composed of more than five volunteer households (one of them must be suffering from poverty or damages caused by elephants). Each household invested 100 RMB to join the fund, and together, they formulated the management measures to ensure that the mutual aid fund was used for productive investment. At the same time, the project also provided villagers with training in agricultural technology, safety education, animal and habitat protection, and carried out rich and colorful environmental education activities in local communities and elementary and middle schools. While protecting Asian elephants, the project improves people's ability to protect their property from wild animals and achieves the goal of harmonious coexistence between humans and elephants.

The investigation team also visited the villages of Shangzhai, Hejiazhai, and Laodongzhai in Nanping Township where the damages caused by elephants were more serious. The wild elephants had just stopped by the village farmland a few days before the team's arrival. The ridges were crushed, sweet bamboo was broken, oranges and tea were trampled, and feces were seen everywhere. On Dawei Mountain, the investigation team saw a newly built pool, which was the source of drinking water for the three villages. The original pool was ruined by elephants not long ago, and the villagers rebuilt the pool to make it more solid, but there was no guarantee that the new pool could survive the wild elephants' visits.

Following the elephants' path, the investigation team climbed over the Dawei Mountain to its south slope. There is a wide river valley. In the rainy season, it provides abundant water sources for agriculture on both banks. But due to the frequent presence of wild elephants, these fertile farmlands have long been abandoned. In the upper part of the valley, the IFAW has built an artificial nitrite pond for wild elephants to bathe and obtain salt. It was said that wild elephants came soon after the nitrite pond was built.

When the investigation team saw the village out of the mountain stream, they were struck with the realization that the range of wild elephants was gradually increasing while the range of human activities was gradually shrinking.

A Magic Telepathy between Hearts

Based on their four-day investigation, long-term data collection, and repeated exchanges with experts, the investigation team came to the conclusion that the ultimate goal of wild elephant protection is to achieve peaceful coexistence. Human beings can choose their ways of living, but elephants have to follow their instincts. To this end, the members of the investigation team put forward some solutions to the human-elephant conflicts in combination with their own thinking, for example, the Preliminary Investigation on Insurance Compensation and Mitigation of Human-elephant Conflicts in Simao, the Investigation Report on Human-elephant Conflicts in Simao: the Idea of Building an Ecological Corridor in the Asian Elephant Activity Area in Simao, The Plan and Suggestions on Tourism to Alleviate Human-elephant Conflicts in Simao, the Impact of Nitrite Pond Construction on the Migration Routes and Feeding Behavior of Asian Elephants, and The Impact of the Construction and Restoration of an Ecological Corridor on the Reproduction and Communication of Asian Elephants.

Members of the investigation team recorded their feelings along the way.

Yang Xinzhou originally thought that endangered wild animal protection should come at any price, but after interviewing the villagers and seeing the severely damaged farmland and crops, he formed a new understanding: "We realize that neither sacrificing the interests of humans or the living conditions of elephants is acceptable or even feasible. There is still a long way to go on the path of exploring harmonious development with nature."

"Special love for special you" is a heartfelt remark made by Lü Wei to the five Asian elephants. Although they trampled on farmland and stole food, the local villagers still regard them as mascots and are willing to raise their favorite plants free of charge. Countless volunteers are also working on the frontlines of the elephant-damaged areas for the ultimate purpose of harmonious coexistence. "Here, I see that people's awareness of environmental protection is improving, and I see more and more hope," said Lü.

"Asian elephants are our friends, but they are also the 'culprits' of our great losses." Xie Tinghao said. Through the investigation, he came to the understanding that caring for wildlife should start with caring for people, and that wildlife protection should not be at the expense of human interests. The introduction of this theory brought our understanding of environmental protection to a higher level. Lu Junqi said: "We cannot drive away the people who have lived here for generations in order to protect elephants, nor can we move the elephants for economic interests. Common development is the real solution to the problem."

Advisor Xu Jiulin believed that within a rapidly developing human society, we often forget that human beings are merely one of the thousands of species on the Earth. Other species have the same right to enjoy the beautiful home of the Earth as us. Even if we have the ability, we should not hinder or interfere with the existence of other species that enjoy the equal right to survive on this planet.

Another advisor Ma Yun shared that it was the efforts of a group of caring experts and committed villagers who did not care about personal gains and losses that kept the Asian elephant in Simao. "Verbal promises of protection are too feeble. I hope that one day, the Asian elephants and other wild animals will no longer be labeled 'protected.'"

The four-year animal protection week led to a joint scientific practice. As the organizer of the four-year animal protection week, Mr. Yang Kun felt deeply responsible and gratified. He said, "Our efforts paid off. The ideas we planted in our students' minds have come to fruition." During this event, the students not only understood the humans' need for getting along with nature and animals but also perceived the miracle of lives and the magic telepathy between hearts.

In 2021, the TikTok platform "Cute Yunnan Broadcast" jointly developed by Yunnan Education Foundation and local enterprises contacted the investigation team. Although it has been eighteen years, the sprouts of elephants and biodiversity protection planted by the investigation have blossomed in the hearts of these former students.

Xiao Xuerui, who is now a graduate student majoring in Global Media and Communication through the London School of Economics and Political Science (LSE) and the University of Southern California (USC), shared that the investigative project that year introduced the concept of "environmental protection" to her life. In the following years, she has always paid attention to environmental protection and practiced the concept as a volunteer many times. Yang Xinzhou, who is now the Head of Strategic Investment at a technology company, reflected that the practical project in 2004 was to actively explore how to build an ecological corridor of Asian elephants' habitat; what is needed now is to study and solve the problem of harmonious coexistence between humans and elephants on a higher level. Xie Tinghao, who now engages in commercial real estate management, said that both the government and the public have come a long way in handling human-elephant conflicts. The concept of ecological civilization is guiding people to build a better and more beautiful home for wildlife and human beings.

[Notes: The information included in this chapter is from the data recorded by the nineteen teachers and students from Kunming No. 12 Middle School and the High School Affiliated to Yunnan Normal University on their Asian elephant biodiversity investigation trip to Simao (today's Pu'er), January 14–18, 2004.]

International Fund for Animal Welfare (IFAW)

Founded in 1969, IFAW is one of the largest animal welfare organizations in the world. It aims to improve the welfare of wildlife and companion animals by reducing commercial exploitation and trade, improving wildlife habitat protection, and rescuing animals in distress. The IFAW actively advocates the concept of the harmonious coexistence of human beings and animals and promotes animal welfare and protection policies that benefit all.

The organization has been carrying out projects in China since 1993. In recent years, its main projects in China include the rescue of wild Asian elephants, Tibetan antelopes, and raptors in Beijing.

Cute Yunnan Broadcast

On July 14, 1988, the Yunnan Education Foundation was officially established with the approval of Yunnan Provincial People's Government. As a 5A-level public offering foundation, it aims to "alleviate poverty, support education, help poor students, train and reward teachers, promote the social morality of respecting

111

teachers, valuing education, and the balanced development of poverty alleviation in education in Yunnan."

The "Cute Yunnan Broadcast" is a joint TikTok account created by the Yunnan Provincial Education Foundation and local enterprises to publicize the theme activities of biodiversity in Yunnan. It contextualizes the natural science education, ecological civilization education, ethnic customs education, and urban sustainable development education in elementary and middle schools in Yunnan in the real natural environment, and explores and practices education in the real natural environment supported by the ideology of "read thousands of books and travel thousands of miles." Going deep into nature, "Cute Yunnan Broadcast" helps elementary and middle school students in Yunnan understand the rich biodiversity resources in their hometown, further spreads the awareness of environmental protection, and allows them to effectively improve their practical and innovation ability in biodiversity protection with a broad vision and a comprehensive understanding of life and culture.

Breaking the Shell Nature Education Organization

Founder Zhou Xiuyuan is a nature tutor certified by the Danish Forest Education Association. He is committed to natural science popularization, and he firmly believes that children's awareness of nature protection should be based on science and an in-depth understanding of nature. The Breaking the Shell Nature Education Organization leads the children to learn about the origin and evolution of the elephant species and the changes of the distribution of Asian elephants in China from history, visit Xishuangbanna, the habitat of Asian elephants in China, acquire environmental knowledge in the Xishuangbanna Tropical Botanical Garden of the Chinese Academy of Sciences, ask about the physical structure and behavior habits of elephants in Xishuangbanna Asian Elephant Breeding and Rescue Center, and interview the indigenous people, staff members, and tourists in Xishuangbanna National Nature Reserve to understand different people's positions on the protection of Asian elephants. It is hoped that through the research on the relationship between humans and elephants, children can establish the awareness of a "shared earth" and an ecological civilization of all creatures.

4

The "Sun Birds": Writers Who Tell the Stories of Biodiversity

Yunnan's biodiversity environment provides a nutrient-rich soil for literary creation. At the same time, the literary creation that tells the story of biodiversity and reflects the relationship between humans and nature cultivates the public's ecological values and inspires more people to contribute to the construction of an ecological civilization.

At present, more and more Yunnan writers are paying attention to the local natural ecology and are expanding the realm of their literary creations from people's social life to plants and animals, mountains and rivers, and all living beings and the universe. They disclose the essence of Yunnan's ecological harmony and move numerous readers with their stories.

The Yunnan expression mode of ecological literature creation can be traced back to the 1980s.

At that time, in the field of Yunnan children's literature, a group of writers named the "Sun Birds" caught the public eye. With unique children's perspectives, rich literary styles as well as simple but catchy language, they passionately presented to the world a dazzling wonderland with attractive ethnic cultures.

For thirty years, three generations of "Sun Bird" writers have become the guardian spirits of the innocent world of children on the Yunnan plateau. With broad creative visions and distinctive literary focuses, they told the stories of Yunnan and enriched Chinese children's literature.

The "Elephant Chasers" in the Literary Circle

"As the leading elephant moved, the herd also moved. Hesitantly, they followed it out of the Kuishan Island, lagging behind. At first, the herd was rioting and roaring. They stepped forward, and stepped backward again ..."

"Slowly, the elephants embarked on the road paved with tender bamboo and plantains by Yan Nuonuo and the militia. They greedily gorged on the tender bamboo and wild plantains sprinkled with salt water and gradually calmed down. Then, they marched toward Mengpeng Nature Reserve along the 'happy road' paved by the People's Liberation Army and people of all ethnic groups."

This is from the first short story *When Elephants Migrate* by Shen Shixi, the "king of animal novels" from forty-two years ago. It was based on the true event of Asian elephants' southbound migration that the author experienced while working in Xishuangbanna, Yunnan.

Shen is probably the first "elephant chaser" in the field of children's literature. He has used the Internet name Lao Xiang (old elephant) for many years. He became friends with the elephants, and his elephant stories made him famous. These animals have become part of his life and identity now. He said, "The magical land of Yunnan has nourished my writing. It became a fertile land for my literary creation."

In 1969, Shen graduated from middle school and arrived at Xishuangbanna following the national "down to the countryside" movement. The local customs bred by the tropical rainforest deeply inspired his pursuit of literary creation. Shen recalled, "I saw someone riding an elephant up the mountain to pull wood the first day I arrived at the village." In the late 1970s, a dozen Asian elephants migrated southward in the dense forests of Xishuangbanna, only 100 kilometers away from the China-Laos border. The event was the most "eye-catching" creation material for Shen, who was the publicity secretary at that time. He wrote his first animal novel *When Elephants Migrate* and entered the Chinese literary world.

After living in Yunnan for thirty-six years, the author and "elephant chaser" Shen finished multiple classic works centering on the Asian elephant: *Tears of the Elephant King*, *White Elephant Family*, *Elephant Tomb*, and *The Last War Elephant*. Over the past forty years of writing, Shen's works involving more than fifty kinds of animals have been published with a total of more than five million words and have more than 100 million readers. He shows the "humans and nature" around him in his own way. "This 'old elephant' would not have existed without Yunnan—I can even say that the whole natural ecological pattern in Chinese children's literature today would not have existed without Yunnan."

A Natural World in Every Story

"I love literature, and I like to read a little of everything when I have the time. My eldest daughter turned two in 1972. I wanted to give her a meaningful present, but I couldn't find any in the stores. So I borrowed a *Greek Mythology* from a friend and spent a month copying it by hand with my wife. We gave it to our daughter on her birthday. At that time, I had a dream: I wanted to write books for children."

—*My Thirty Years*, Wu Ran.

Wu Ran is still an evergreen tree in the field of Yunnan's local children's literature after half a century. He is obsessed with children's literature, committed to his readers, and runs through his works with childlike innocence, childlike playfulness, gentility, kindness, and praise for natural beauty.

Wu Ran has more than sixty works selected into elementary and middle school Chinese textbooks, which makes him the most selected author in Yunnan. His famous works such as *The Pearl Spring*, *Our National Minority Elementary School*, *Bayberry Club*, *Walking the Moon*, *That Black-Headed Gull*, *The Little*

Bird and the Old Forest Keeper, and *Peacock Dance* have opened a door to Yunnan and nature for many young readers.

Wu Ran, whose birth name is Wu Xingran, is from Xuanwei, Yunnan. In his biography, Wu recalls his childhood: "Ever since I was a child, I worked in the fields herding cattle, mowing grass, and cutting firewood. I have even worked in the coal mines. Life was very hard back then." He always remembers the scene of his mother tweezing out splinters from his feet and the warmth of her tears falling on his soles; he also remembers the beautiful mountain village, the river and the Longtan pond at the front, and the woods, the birds, the flowers, and the rainbow after the rain at the back ... He loves the deep, humid, and aromatic alleys in Kunming, the waves and sailboats on Dianchi Lake, the snow on Cangshan Mountain, the moon in Erhai Lake, and the colorful ethnic customs left by the ancient Nanzhao kingdom.

Wu Ran has worked as vice-editor of *Chuncheng Evening News* for nearly thirty years, and he was in charge of editing the children's literature journal *Little Orange Lantern*. He wrote to Bing Xin, a famous 20th-century Chinese woman writer and the author of the novel *Little Orange Lantern*, for her handwritten inscription of the title. Wu recalled, "I didn't expect to receive her writing in just a few days. She wrote the three characters both horizontally and vertically, both stamped with her seal."

The memories of the past, especially childhood memories, are Wu's favorite sources of literary creation. His days in Dali left an indelible mark in his life, and he poured his happiness and sorrow into the prose and poetry *A Bowl of Water*, *Brother Tree*, *The Blacksmith in the Village*, *Cow*, and *Lone Pine Tree*. Wu said: "The people and things from my childhood, the life and scenery of my hometown and of Dianchi Lake in Kunming and the Cangshan Mountain and Erhai Lake in Dali, and everything I have seen and visited in the frontier ethnic minority areas, all come to life before my eyes. I began to appreciate the beauty of life with the eyes and the hearts of children."

Wu said he liked the simple, natural kind of beauty, and he liked himself being the childlike, innocent "flower whisperer" in the eyes of his friend. So he weaves this simple and natural beauty into his works. He takes children to see the small flowers by the road, to watch the black-headed gulls in winter, to feel the mountains and the waters in Yunnan, and to embrace the natural ecology of harmonious coexistence.

A Group of Authors' Re-Exploration of the Natural Ecology of Yunnan

Yunnan's unique biodiversity resources provide writers with unlimited creative natural soil.

After entering this beautiful, magical, rich and colorful land, writers dig and discover the poetic secret Yunnan in the form of literature. As the "leading birds" of the "Sun Birds," Shen Shixi, Qiao Chuanzao, Wu Ran, Chen Yuehong, Yu Lei, Shen Tao, Tang Ping, and other writers in Yunnan have created a new world with their individual writing style in children's literature.

Qiao Chuanzao's essays on forests and animals pursue the harmony between humans and nature; Shen Shixi's animal novels examine the human world and the animal world at the same level, setting up a banner of ecological literature for Yunnan. In Tang Ping's view, good children's literature should not only reflect the contemporary time but also go beyond its limit to build a world with rich levels. Wu Ran said, "The era when we can only get the impression of Yunnan from a large number of literary works has passed. The writing posture of the new generation 'Sun Birds' is more open, the writing themes are more modern, and the creative techniques are more diverse. We no longer excessively emphasize our national identity and regional characteristics but pay attention to the world, the present, and the environment with a broader vision." By now, many writers in the group of "Sun Birds" are still committed to telling the story of biodiversity in Yunnan and making efforts for children to understand and protect the natural ecology.

Yu Lei thinks that "Ecological literature is one of the themes of today's world literature," of which ecological children's literature is an important branch. Its importance both reflects the need of the times and society and the product of the real environment.

The Oral History of Yunnan Ecological Children's Literature Writers, written by Li Xiu'er, is the first written work on this topic in China. It shows us the broad subject field and aesthetic space for the development of children's literature provided by Yunnan's unique natural environmental resources.

The poet Xiao Xue spoke highly of this oral history, saying that it drew on the latest theoretical achievements of eco-centrism and ecological literature research, "Taking the overall interests of the ecosystem as the highest value, investigates and expresses the relationship between nature and human beings, explores the social root of the ecological crisis, expresses the ideal of harmonious coexistence between human beings and all things in nature, and navigates the path for Yunnan children's literature from the height of ecological civilization so as to open the door to explore natural ecology for its future development."

Plant the Seeds of Ecological Protection into the Hearts of All Children in the World

Ever since the 1980s, the creation of ecological children's literature in Yunnan has had a unique impact in the country, and the "Sun Bird" writers have made remarkable achievements. Yunnan children's literature writers have always kept pace with the world in the exploration of ecological harmony.

On the eve of the October First National Day in 2021, at the award ceremony of the Eleventh National Excellent Children's Literature Award in Beijing, the story *I Want to Grow into a Tree* by Yunnan writer Chen Yuehong (whose pseudonym is Xiang Nü) was the only work that won the prize. This was also a successful attempt by Yunnan writers to imperceptibly cultivate children's ecological consciousness and guide readers to think and explore the harmonious coexistence between humans and nature through literary forms. The constant support of Yunnan children's literature not only provides nutrients for the field in the whole country but also adds color to that in the world.

For example, Wu Ran, who is affectionately known as the "lantern holder" of Yunnan children's literature, not only enlightens the world of innocence for Chinese children but also brightens the childhood of children all over the world. His work *New Year's Gift* was selected into a bilingual textbook for the third graders in South Korea and the Kumon textbook in Japan that is used in more than forty countries.

Today, Yunnan's achievements in biodiversity conservation have gained worldwide attention and recognition. There is no doubt that these lovely "Sun Bird" writers will continue in their literary creations, to tell the story of Yunnan, where man and nature harmoniously coexist through colorful childlike innocence.

The "Sun Birds" Writing Group

The name "Sun Birds" is a poetic metaphor for the basic trend of Yunnan children's literature creation and the unique aesthetic pursuit of its writers. The first group of "Sun Birds" included Liu Qi, Yang Meiqing, Ma Ruilin, Nie Suo, and Zhao Kewen, as well as Li Qiao, Peng Jingfeng, Xiao Xue, Li Junlong, Yang Mingyuan, Sun Jibin, and Zhu Depu, who wrote for children at different periods. The "Sun Birds" writing group was finally formed thanks to a large number of writers including Shen Shixi, Qiao Chuanzao, Wu Ran, Wu Tian, Yan Tingting, Ning Xi, and more. In recent years, the legacy of the "Sun Birds" has been carried forward by young and middle-aged writers such as Chen Yuehong, Yang Baozhong, Tang Ping, Yu Lei, Zeng Yanping, and Liu Jiachen.

Wu Ran explained the connotation of "Sun Birds" as thus—"Sun birds! The light-and-freedom-loving sun birds, like flying flowers, fly in the colorful sky of Yunnan. Fly high, sing proudly, and be something different in contemporary Chinese children's literature."

5

The Power of Image in Protecting
a Harmonious Ecology

If we want to find a carrier for biodiversity that connects nature, scientific research, the public, and the government, then it must be an image. A group of people are recording, popularizing science, and protecting ecology through images in the mountains, by the water, and among the clouds. They are ecological photographers—they use images to reflect the relationships between various organisms, between organisms and the environment, and between humans and nature to publicize the magical and beautiful natural ecosystem and rich biodiversity.

Xi Zhinong is the most well-known Yunnan photographer active in the field of ecological photography with thirty-eight years of experience in wildlife photography. He believes there are still many "wild places" in China with much unique natural wildlife in the world, but what appears before the public is still very limited. In 2002, Xi established the "Wild China" studio and determined to protect nature with images. Likewise, Fan Yi, an ecological photographer in Yunnan, has also been committed to photographing the cultural landscape and the beauty of biodiversity in Western China, especially in Yunnan.

With their camera lens, the ecological photographers create a stage for every creature in the vast world, showing the individuals and groups of the earth's biodiversity or a new starting point of species evolution. By recording vivid images of wild animals and plants, they arouse more attention and protection of biodiversity in public.

Record in Nature

After "hiding away" for eighty-seven years, *Meconopsis georgei* finally appeared again.

Fan Yi made a crucial contribution to its reappearance.

Meconopsis georgei (*angiosperms, papaveraceae, meconopsis*), is a species native to the Northwest Yunnan and mostly grows on screes, the collection of broken rock fragments at the base of a cliff that has accumulated through periodic rockfall. British plant hunters had collected plant specimens of *Meconopsis georgei* as early as July 1931. However, since then, the plant has "mysteriously disappeared" and no experts or scholars have collected any *Meconopsis georgei* similar to model specimens.

On August 5, 2018, Fan Yi and Wei Lai, a botanist from Beijing Normal University went to Biluo Mountain to shoot and collect plant specimens. Fan recalled that when they struggled over the mountain pass, his attention was completely attracted by a plant of *Meconopsis* he had never seen before. He said, "I joked with Mr. Wei that there was a *Meconopsis georgei* here."

Fan did not expect that research later proved that this was indeed a *Meconopsis georgei*.

Again, in 2018, Yunnan reported a new record of amphibian—the *Theloderma gordoni*. In fact, Fan Yi had already photographed this tree frog in 2015.

"I went to a very ordinary river to take pictures of insects, but I saw this very strange tree frog. I have never seen that kind of color before, especially the light blue on its body that looks like green roof tiles." The experienced ecological photographer keenly judged that this tree frog may be a new species.

Through Fan's camera lens, we see many plants and animals in the "Digital Encyclopedia of Biodiversity in Yunnan." Whether the *Ottelia acuminata* (a species of aquatic plant) in the water, the *Androsace mollis* (a species of flower) in the forest, the *Rheum alexandrae* (a tall ornamental rhubarb plant) in the mountains, or the *Arguda insulindiana* (a species of moth) perching on dead leaves, the *Theloderma bicolor* (a species of frog) hiding under the moss, the fierce *Odontomachus circulus* (a species of omnivorous ants) ... all creatures in Yunnan are given an opportunity to shine in Fan's lens.

For three nights, he photographed *Camponotus nicobarensis* (a species of ants) frantically attacking weevils, termite breeding ants, and even their "close relative" *Odontomachus monticola Emery*; he noticed that *Primula chionantha* (the snow-white primrose, a species of flowering plant) can look slightly differently at different altitudes and habitats, and even though he has captured many photos of it, he is sure that his next picture will be distinctive; when he first saw the *Elatostema salvinioides* (a perennial herb), he was completely fascinated as he marveled at its unworldly beauty ...

Like a traveler on a long journey, Fan Yi is always looking forward to new surprises on the road as an ecological photographer.

Extremely Beautiful and Dangerous

Fan Yi has many identities—Vice-President of the Association for the Protection and Promotion of Yunnan Natural and Cultural Heritage, core member of Images Biodiversity Expedition (IBE), special photographer of China National Geography, and founder of VANMO Photography Studio, and more.

Since 2010, Fan Yi has been to more than sixty national protected areas and depopulated zones and photographed wild animals, plants, and natural land-scapes, mainly in Western China. He goes to the "Three Parallel Rivers" area in Yunnan every year. Even the tiniest and most insignificant insects and mimicry creatures display the striking beauty of nature in their own special ways. "I liked to play with insects a lot when I was a child. Later, I found another side of insects through a macro lens, something we can't see with the naked eye." After studying advertising in college, Fan became a communication systems engineer. In order to alleviate the pressure from this complicated and stressful job, Fan bought an SLR camera like many others at the time and began to shoot insects.

Once, Fan and his friends went to Napahai Lake in Shangri-La region of Yunnan. "All those birds soared into the air together—there were about two or three thousand—and their cries echoed above the Napahai Lake." Fan was absolutely stunned and felt as if he was in the French documentary *Winged Migration*. Something he had never dared to think about came up in his mind. Later, he quit his job and prepared to become a full-time ecological photographer. He still remembers the stares from his colleagues when he left the office, who said, "Old Fan is definitely possessed."

After his resignation, Fan had no fixed income, but he had to spend money on equipment, field shooting, and post production. In order to make a living, Fan had to make some commercial shoots, but he always knew that this was not his pursuit. "I love ecology. I think it is a power of social values and with a sense of mission."

Starting from little insects, the frame of Fan's photography began to grow. "I take pictures of all ecological types—insects, amphibians, reptiles, birds, mammals, and alpine plants." Fan frankly said that an ecological photographer both needs photographic technology and a certain level of biological literacy. Every time he photographed an unknown biological species, Fan would check out about it online or consult experts. His commitment to continuous learning enabled him to shoot excellent work.

Once, Fan was invited to Wenshan, Yunnan to shoot *Magnolia sinica*, the oldest endangered plant of Magnoliaceae with the least preserved quantity in the world. The plant can reach a height of more than forty meters, and it blooms once every one to two years. Just as Fan was amazed by the gorgeous flowering scene of the *Magnolia sinica*, a gust of wind and rain suddenly hit. Fan and other photographers quickly packed up their cameras to take shelter from the rain. But when the rain stopped, they found that the petals had been ruined by the hail, so they shifted to another plant.

"My face was actually very close to it, but I didn't notice until the girl behind me said that there was a frog." It was a *Theloderma bicolor* that Fan was referring to. Following the girl's instruction, Fan noticed a frog lying on the moss in the tree hole. As the top "camouflage master" in nature, the *Theloderma bicolor* grows significantly raised wart particles all cover its skin through mimicry evolution that makes it look like the moss on the trunk. With its body color similar to the moss, the *Theloderma bicolor* almost merges completely into the surrounding environment, making it very difficult to be spotted. After that, the academic community confirmed that the *Theloderma bicolor* was a new species in Yunnan. Fan Yi is probably the first in Yunnan and even in China to photograph the *Theloderma bicolor*.

The "Defender of Wildlife Images"

Fan Yi takes many pictures of rare alpine plants in Yunnan. His images bring to the world the wonderful creatures who live in the inaccessible, four-to-five thousand kilometers high mountains. The portraits of these rare animals and plants not only provided the public enjoyment of beauty but also shaped the concept of an ecological civilization that called for people's awareness of environmental protection. But for ecological photographers, extreme beauty often comes with extreme dangers.

Fan can never forget the thrilling experience of looking for *Amolops* (a genus of frog).

It was already dark, but Fan still decided to go to the spot where they were shooting. With a flashlight in his hand, he walked for a long time and saw an unseen frog on a big rock. Fan recalled, "Just then, I missed a step and fell off." There was a puddle below, about three meters away from the rock. The water pushed Fan into the puddle. "There was a lot of water. It kept running on me, and I couldn't get up at all. I thought I might die." Fan was washed down and choked by the water, but he soon calmed himself and tried to step on a rock so that he could hold his head out of the water and breathe. Then he turned on the flashlight and called to his friends for help. Fortunately, Fan was finally saved, and he still didn't forget to look for the frog.

Fan has won a dozen awards in the International Garden Photographer of the Year competition, including three runners-up. He has also won all the highest awards in the domestic natural ecology photography competitions since 2014. June, July, and August are the most important field shooting months for Fan. During this time, he goes to the mountains to look for rare plateau plants. Fan said, "We hope to inspire people's awareness in environmental protection by capturing the beautiful sceneries and lovely creatures with our cameras."

Among all his awards, Fan is most proud of the "Defender of Wildlife Images" awarded by the Sixth Wildlife Defender Award Ceremony, which may be the best description of his career. "He has walked 30,000 miles and visited nearly 50 nature reserves in China. With his camera, he recorded more than 2,000 species in China, including 41 species of mammals, 380 species of birds, 27 species of reptiles, 43 species of amphibians, more than 1,000 species of insects, more than 750 species of higher plants, more than 50 species of fungi, and more than 10 species of lichens. Thank you, for protecting China, and for your continuous efforts and contributions to protect alpine plant species unique to China, especially the Hengduan Mountains in the southwest."

Images Biodiversity Expedition (IBE)

With rich biological knowledge and solid photographic aesthetic foundation, ecological photographers of the Images Biodiversity Expedition apply various technical means such as long lens shooting, macro and micro shots, underwater shots, infrared trigger shots, and camera GPS positioning to record natural moments with both aesthetic value and scientific research value. IBE has created a new photography action: a group of natural photographers with strong background in natural history gather together to restore the biodiversity of an area in three dimensions. In this way, they hope to form a database of China's natural image annals.

Digital Encyclopedia of Biodiversity in Yunnan

On New Year's Day in 2020, Yunnan Daily Newspaper Group planned and launched the publicity event "Digital Encyclopedia of Biodiversity in Yunnan." The event solicited photography works from domestic well-known ecological photographers to show the effectiveness of Yunnan's ecological civilization construction and the beauty of biodiversity in Yunnan, and released a total of 308 beautiful local species. Twenty-three photographers traveled to the dense forests, the screes (collection of broken rock fragments at the base of a cliff or other steep rocky mass that has accumulated through periodic rockfall) at an altitude of 5,000 meters, and the inaccessible mountains and valleys to record the best looks of these lives with their cameras.

CHAPTER 4

The Simplest Words Convey the Greatest Truth

"COVID-19 reminds us of the interdependence between man and nature. It falls to all of us to act together and urgently to advance protection and development in parallel, so that we can turn Earth into a beautiful homeland for all creatures to live in harmony."

—In September 2020, President Xi Jinping delivered an important speech via video at the UN Summit on Biodiversity.

"Lucid waters and lush mountains are invaluable assets. A sound ecology and environment is not just a natural asset, but also an economic asset, and it affects the potential and momentum of economic and social development. We need to speed up efforts to foster a green way of development and secure a win-win of economic growth and environmental protection, so as to build a homeland of coordinated advancement of economy and the environment."

—On the afternoon of October 12, 2021, President Xi Jinping attended the leaders' summit of the 15th meeting of the Conference of the Parties to the Convention on Biological Diversity (COP15) held in Kunming via video link and delivered a keynote speech.

The story of the Short Trunks is an amazing Chinese story that took place in a new era. It highlighted China's actions and achievements in the fields of environmental and biodiversity protection, reflecting China's wisdom, experience, and practices. More importantly, it vividly delineated the image of an eastern superpower that loves nature and advocates harmony. For China and all countries in the world, a profound lesson was learned. Nature is the basic condition for human survival and development. It gives birth to human beings, and thus humans should respect, accommodate, and protect nature as their roots.

1

The Footnotes of Love for Elephants

Many literary and artistic works on the theme of Asian elephants have been published in order to better tell the story of the Short Trunks and influence more people. They constantly excavate the meanings of Yunnan elephants' journey to and from the north and expand its extension as much as possible. In a way, these works are building a super "Asian elephant IP" which can play a very positive role in forming self-awareness of animal protection and the popularity of the concept of environmental protection.

Hold the Elephants in Our "Hands"

How do we hold the giant elephants in our hands?

The answer is: write books for them. On "World Elephant Day," the two earliest books on the story of the Short Trunks were officially published in China: *Cute Elephants Love Yunnan* and *Travel Notes of Wild Elephants in Yunnan*. Why write books for elephants? In writers' view, the Short Trunks are so lovely and their journey is so interesting. How meaningful it will be to hold a book about them in our hands and read their stories!

Motivated by this thought, the main authors of different industries, age groups, and identities gathered together. After many times of brainstorming, framing, text polishing, picture selecting, communicating, and negotiating, these two books with far-reaching ideas, dual purposes in education and entertainment, and strong readability finally met with their readers.

What makes the books special is the first-person narrative written from the perspectives of the Short Trunks when telling the interesting and embarrassing stories the elephants encountered in their travel. "They" talk about the local customs they see and recall the unforgettable friendship they formed with their human protectors. It makes the books both fun and heartwarming to read.

As the first "elephant book" introduced to the public, *Cute Elephants Love Yunnan* and *Travel Notes of Wild Elephants in Yunnan* also brought rare, high-quality photos of the Short Trunks aside from the beautifully written stories. Hundreds of precious pictures showing the elephant herd sleeping together on their backs, taking mud baths, turning on water taps, playing in the cornfield, and wandering with garlands on their trunks were included in the books and shown to the public for the first time.

Famous writer of children's literature Wu Ran is very fond of these books, and he recommends them to more readers. He said, "I believe these two books will bring rich and beautiful reading enjoyment to all readers, including children."

Write Elephants a Song

Music can quickly find an echo with people, especially when the subject of the song is a baby elephant. It touches the softest part of one's heart.

Little elephant, little baby elephant, you are a cute big baby
Little elephant, little baby elephant, you are a brave big baby
Your trunk is so long; your ears are so big
You chubby, cuddly baby, run around and play
......

On August 12, 2021, the excellent children's folk song *Little Baby Elephant*, with rich cultural, national, ecological, and popular elements, was presented as the opening song in the *Focus On* program of CCTV 13. With simple and easy-to-remember lyrics and catchy tunes, it became a popular song just a few days after it was broadcast.

"You can't forget it after hearing it just once." This is what the audience generally feels about the *Little Baby Elephant*. Its simple and vivid lyrics as well as the lively music style coupled with cucurbit flute (or *hulusi*, a flute made from a gourd), *bawu* flute (a bamboo traverse flute) and other national minority musical instruments impress the audience with the special melody from the Xishuangbanna tropical rainforest, making it a truly unforgettable enjoyable auditory experience.

The lyric of the song was written by Wen Xing, a Yunnan media worker and vice-president of the Kunming Literary Critics Association, and the music was composed by Zhang Wendong, Director of the radio and television station at Qiubei County, Wenshan Prefecture. The inspiration of the creation of the song comes from an "elephant salon" that brings together industry experts to explore how to protect Asian elephants and the ecological environment in Yunnan. The serious meeting atmosphere and the lively music style of the finished song formed a strong contrast. Everyone was curious as to why Wen and Zhang wrote a children's folk rhyme.

What Wen had in mind was how to pass the idea of Asian elephant protection to children when the whole world is talking about individual participation in these projects. Wen's original thought was, "We made this folk rhyme for children, and we wanted to plant the 'seeds' of protecting elephants, wild animals, and nature into the hearts of young children."

Make Elephants a Sculpture

Sculpture is the art of capturing and passing through time. Naturally, to memorize the epic story of the Short Trunks, the famous artist Yuan Xikun's elephant-themed sculpture came into being.

Yuan was born in Kunming. Aside from his fabulous achievement in the field of sculpture, he has a wide range of interests and has also been committed to environmental protection. He has been paying attention to the Plateau Mingzhu Dianchi Lake, Fuxian Lake, and Yelang Lake for a long time.

Yuan was deeply touched by the wild Asian elephants' "decisive" characteristic. He said: "My home, Yunnan Province, has a unique climate, and I like it as well as the elephants do." His inspirations constantly emerged. He decided to do something and leave something behind.

At that time, Yuan was invited to create a theme sculpture for COP15. He believed that his work should not only reflect the beautiful vision of harmonious coexistence between humans and nature but also show China's responsibility in the field of environmental and biological protection in the world today. There were no better models than the Short Trunks.

After more than 100 days and nights of polishing, Yuan's sculpture was shown in COP15 exhibition hall. It was a 2.39-meter-long, 0.96-meter-wide, and 0.63-meter-high sculpture of the elephant herd titled *The Great Wall Ridge of Lives*. In every little detail, from the tip of the trunk to the tail, from the ears to the toes, from the eyes to the tusks, we can see the tremendous effort and affection poured in by the sculptor that made the work a masterpiece.

Make Elephants a Documentary

During the Short Trunks' journey, "elephant chasers" came from all over the world to record their wonderful and unforgettable moments with UAVs and cameras.

In June 2021, the Film and TV Drama Documentary Center of China Media Group sent two production teams to "chase the elephants" with the Yunnan Provincial Forest Fire Brigade in the frontline. Following the elephants, they obtained a large number of authentic materials and recorded the whole process of the elephant herd's northbound migration. After about two months, the CCTV presented an eight-episode documentary called *A Mammoth Task*, showing the touching, in-depth stories of humans and nature. At a time when we are praising nature with awe and thinking about whether we can approach elephants from an equal perspective, the documentary suggests to us a new ideology—while human beings are trying to find a way to live in harmony with all lives in nature, all lives in nature are also looking for a way to live in harmony with human beings.

On October 11, at the opening ceremony of COP15 at Kunming Dianchi Lake International Convention and Exhibition Center, the documentary *Elephants' Journey in Yunnan* was shown to the guests for the first time. The documentary reconstructed the much-watched journey of the Short Trunks, and it interpreted the ecological wisdom and Chinese understanding of harmonious coexistence between humans and nature in an innovative way.

2

China: Leader of Biodiversity

Did the Short Trunks really miss COP15?

Not necessarily. Although the Short Trunks left Kunming early, they "spiritually" participated in COP15. The sculptures, murals, and creative products inside and outside COP15 venue were all created based on their images; there were many interviews and salons about elephants going on; many officials and even country leaders mentioned them in their speeches.

People made no secret of their love for the Short Trunks, and they highly praised the connotation of the ecological value behind their story. Let's return to the COP15 venue and see how the elephants won everyone's heart.

On the afternoon of October 11, 2021, more than 5,000 representatives from 140 parties and 30 international institutions and organizations attended COP15 at the Kunming Dianchi Lake International Convention and Exhibition Center in Yunnan Province to discuss practical actions for biodiversity conservation.

The Convention on Biological Diversity is one of the international environmental conventions with the largest number of member states in the world. At present, among the 196 parties, China was one of the first subscribers. The Conference of the Parties is the highest deliberative and decision-making mechanism of the Convention on Biological Diversity. It convenes every two years.

In 2010, COP10 was held in Nagoya, Japan. It formulated the Aichi Targets, the global biodiversity conservation goals for the years 2011 to 2020.

Unfortunately, by 2020, none of the twenty Aichi Targets was fully achieved. Only six were partially accomplished.

Under this context, COP15 was closely watched by the world. China's ecological protection construction developed fast in recent years. Following the ideas such as "a sound ecosystem is essential for the prosperity of civilization," "harmonious coexistence between humans and nature," and "view mountains, rivers, forests, farmlands, lakes, grasslands, and deserts are a community of life," can the world learn from the Chinese concept and scheme to reverse the trend of biodiversity loss? Can the Chinese ecological beliefs derived from the ancient wisdom of "all beings flourish when they live in harmony and receive nourishment from nature" and the scientific concept of "lucid waters and lush mountains are invaluable assets" contribute to the world's ecological development?

The Responsibility of a Superpower in COP15

Because of COVID-19, the original Conference, which was scheduled for from October 15 to 28, 2020, was held in two sessions. The first session was held from October 11 to 15, 2021 in a hybrid manner, and the second session to be held in person in the first half of 2022.

The "hard-won" conference fully demonstrated the Chinese government's firm determination to overcome various difficulties and accelerate global biodiversity governance with the international community. It also demonstrated China's responsibility as a superpower.

The theme of the Conference was "Ecological Civilization: Building a Shared Future for All Life on Earth." This was the first time the United Nations held a global conference on this topic. The Kunming Declaration and other important achievements adopted by the Conference have pointed out the direction and gathered consensus for the future global biodiversity protection. In five days,

Chinese and international media reported on the various agendas of COP15 including the opening ceremony, the high-level meeting, and the ecological civilization forum. Pictures, audio and videos transmitted the beautiful vision of global biodiversity protection through newspapers, television, and the Internet across continents.

At this moment, Kunming stood on the global stage and China became the focus of global attention.

Draw the New Blueprint of Global Biodiversity Protection Planning

In recent years, China has continuously promoted biodiversity protection and created a unique path with Chinese characteristics. The international community hopes that China's efforts will play a leading role in global biodiversity conservation in the future.

COP15 hosted by and held in China lived up to the high expectations with fruitful achievements. On the evening of October 15, 2021, the first session of COP15 closed in Kunming. Its characteristics and achievements were reported at the press conference.

The high-level meeting adopted the Kunming Declaration, which gathered a broad consensus and laid a solid foundation for convening the second session of the meeting and formulating the Post-2020 Global Biodiversity Framework. The conference systematically summarized the experience of the international community in biodiversity conservation, promoted the formulation of global biodiversity conservation strategies for the next ten years or longer, and planned a new blueprint for global biodiversity conservation. These very important measures critical to curbing and reversing the severe situation of biodiversity loss and promoting global sustainable development have attracted extensive global attention.

As one of the main outcomes of the Conference, the Kunming Declaration jointly adopted by the parties promised to ensure the formulation, acceptation, and implementation of an effective Post-2020 Global Biodiversity Framework to lay a foundation for the full realization of the vision of harmonious coexistence between humans and nature in 2050.

At the Conference, China also announced a number of new measures for biodiversity protection: China will take the lead in investing 1.5 billion RMB to establish the Kunming Biodiversity Fund, officially set up the first national parks, gradually implement a series of support and guarantee measures for "peak carbon dioxide emissions" in key areas and industries to build a "1 + N" policy system for carbon peaking and carbon neutralization.

Contributing Chinese Wisdom in Biodiversity

"This is a successful conference," said Elizabeth Mrema, executive secretary of Secretariat of the United Nations for the Convention on Biological Diversity. The first session of COP15 had a clear political commitment that will lay a promising foundation for the formulation of the Post-2020 Global Biodiversity Framework at the second session.

Mrema believes that "China has become a global leader in biodiversity and will continue to play a leading role in this regard." China is sharing its efforts and achievements in biodiversity conservation with other parts of the world. These experiences are worth learning from, emulating, and popularizing based on regional situations.

Executive Director of the United Nations Environment Programme Inger Andersen considered the first session of COP15 critical in a way that "it has gathered the consensus of all parties and demonstrated the firm determination of the international community to protect biodiversity."

Since the 1980s, Andersen has visited China multiple times and witnessed the huge development in economic and social realms. Anderson spoke highly of China's achievements in the construction of ecological civilization: "China has done a lot of solid work in environmental governance, and the overall social awareness of environmental protection is increasing." She also expressed her deep appreciation for the concept of "lucid waters and lush mountains are invaluable assets" as "highly strategic and poetic." According to Anderson, in China, the concepts of green, low-carbon, and sustainable development have been reflected in the process of building a modern infrastructure and energy system. With political support, more and more industries are joining the construction of an ecological civilization, contributing valuable experience to that of global construction.

Achim Steiner, Administrator of the United Nations Development Programme, also spoke highly of China's achievements in ecological protection and was gratified by the widespread environmental protection actions in China. He thanked China for hosting this meeting at a critical time, when the earth is facing a major ecological crisis.

Steiner said he was "extremely looking forward" to this conference. He said all lives on earth and the foundation on which all economies depend were "suffering from serious damage." The world was eager for a global biodiversity protection framework from the Conference to motivate all countries to strive for positive environmental protection. It is an urgent and arduous task that can only succeed via strengthened international cooperation.

3

Ecological Civilization: China in the Lead

After the successful opening of COP15 in Kunming, former Secretary General of the United Nations and former Executive Director of the United Nations Environment Programme Erik Solheim talked about the unanimous adoption of The Paris Agreement at the United Nations Climate Change Conference in Paris six years ago.

China's Achievements in Ecological Civilization Construction Are Seen by All

In December 2015, Solheim celebrated his 61st birthday as Chairman of the Development Assistance Committee of the United Nations Organization for economic cooperation and development. He was most impressed by the efforts made by China among the nearly two hundred contracting parties.

In Solheim's view, the Chinese delegation played a very important role in the adoption of the detailed rules for the Paris Agreement. He recalled that during the Conference, he had many late-night meetings with Xie Zhenhua, then China's special representative for climate change. They slept very little and had to drink a lot of espressos to stay awake.

Solheim had many new discoveries after the successful first session of COP15. He saw China's practical actions in building clean energy. "Now, China is a global leader in many green technologies." This was Solheim's heartfelt speech. In July 2021, China issued the Guidelines for Green Development of Foreign Investment and Cooperation emphasizing the need to protect the natural environment in overseas investment. Two months later, China announced at the UN General Assembly its withdrawal from overseas coal-fired power projects, which injected a boost to the global collective response to climate change.

Solheim said: "China's decision will undoubtedly bring huge benefits to biodiversity conservation in the world and it will promote the development of environmental protection technologies along the Belt and Road Initiative route."

By July 2021, China has basically completed the demarcation of the national ecological protection red line, which stipulated that the area proportion of the protection red line should not be less than 25% of the national land area. This was very important for the healthy development of the ecosystem and biodiversity.

The "red line" provides a solution for protecting the most endangered natural environment. Although it is a measure based on local scenarios in China, Solheim considers it having strong referential significance, saying, "It can be the best practice for other countries to learn from and help countries around the world to solve the problem of how to live in harmony with nature."

Solheim acknowledged China's contributions over the years to help steadily increase the population of many rare and endangered wild animals like the giant pandas, Asian elephants, and Tibetan antelopes. In addition to wildlife protection, China has also used artificial breeding technology to pull species such as wild horses and elk back from the brink of extinction.

In addition to the restoration of endangered animal populations, Solheim also mentioned China's achievements and determination in afforestation—an important part of a series of actions to achieve carbon neutrality by 2060. In order to cope with climate change and better protect natural habitats, China will add 36,000 square kilometers of forests every year through 2025. Solheim said: "This figure may not be so intuitive. Let's just say that China's annual green area is bigger than the territory of Belgium."

Witness the Changes of China's Natural Environment

Erik Solheim has a long history with China. He visited China for the first time in 1984, and he remembered it as being poorer than most countries in Africa. "At that time, there were no private cars or high-speed railways in China. There was only one subway line in Beijing.

But China's later development astonished him. Now, China is one of the most modern countries on Earth, with leading technology, a rapidly expanding economy, and comprehensive accomplishments in poverty alleviation. China has 40,000 kilometers of green high-speed rail, while the United States has zero. Solheim believes that China has very successfully dealt with the biggest challenge of the twentieth century—development, and it is now working hard to conquer the biggest challenge in the twenty-first century—the construction of an ecological civilization.

A set of data supports his view. In 2020, China provided half of the world's solar energy. China is by far the world's largest producer of wind energy and a world leader in green hydrogen.

Seventy percent of the world's high-speed rail and 99% of the electric buses are in China. In 2020, China took up 40% of the global electric vehicle market. At present, the scale of subways in Beijing and Shanghai has entered the forefront of the world. More than thirty-five Chinese cities have effective, clean, and cheap subway systems.

Solheim has been in China many times since his first visit, and he has witnessed the huge changes that took place in environmental protection and ecological restoration in this country. In April 2018, Solheim visited the rural areas of Pujiang, Anji, and other places in Zhejiang Province.

In the past, due to the neglect of water treatment and disorderly emission, the local river was seriously polluted and even showed a muddy, "milkish" color. Since the local government's implementation of the "river chief system" and serious environmental remediation, the river has returned to its normal look. At the same time, the locals adopted the development model of a circular economy. All kinds of waste were reused and wetlands were protected. Fish and birds came back again, and the local residents enjoyed a higher-quality living environment. With a better ecological environment, tourism made great progress which brought huge economic development opportunities.

Solheim said, "In a relatively short time, Zhejiang has achieved environmental governance results that have taken decades for some western countries." This shows Zhejiang's determination and wisdom to promote environmental governance and build an ecological civilization.

Three months later, Solheim went to Hebei Province to visit Saihanba. In December 2017, he awarded the "Earth Guardian Award," the highest honor of the United Nations environmental protection, to the builders of Saihanba forest farm on behalf of the United Nations. After three generations' arduous struggle, this once cold and barren land is now green and flourishing. He said: "The current Saihanba is like a green Great Wall that is blocking the Hunshandak Desert from advancing southward. This is a great example of combining poverty alleviation with environmental restoration and protection."

Solheim also paid attention to the effectiveness of controlling the Kubuqi Desert in Inner Mongolia. At the Seventh Kubuqi International Desert Forum held in July 2021, Solheim highly praised the "Kubuqi experience" as excellent even by international standards. "In Kubuqi, you can see green mountains and people eliminating poverty. It's a win-win situation in Kubuqi, thanks to a good political environment, policies, and enterprises. The 'Kubuqi experience' tells us that a desert can generate electricity and provide renewable and tourism resources. Therefore, the desert is a potential advantage and opportunity for the well-being and health of humanity."

The "Kubuqi experience" should be shared, in order to turn problems into opportunities. According to Solheim: "The 'Kubuqi experience' shows that desert has the potential to develop large-scale economy ... we have empirical evidence that proved the 'Kubuqi model' is realizable and replicable. We should introduce it to other parts of the whole world, such as Nigeria and Morocco."

China's Experience in Promoting the Construction of an Ecological Civilization Is Worth Popularizing

Erik Solheim often said that the world needs China's leadership to embark on a new journey of global ecological civilization. The concept of "lucid waters and lush mountains are invaluable assets" is affecting China and the world. It made the many opportunities brought by green development, such as increasing employment, promoting the economy, and creating a better future for mankind visible to more people.

These Chinese experiences include the desert control in Inner Mongolia, Xinjiang, and Gansu Provinces, as well as the green city construction in the city of Shenzhen, Hangzhou, and the Xiong'an New Area (in Baoding, Hebei Province). In addition, the Belt and Road Initiative (BRI) is also developing toward a "greener" direction, making it an important carrier of the construction of the earth's ecological civilization. The Initiative is of great significance to tackling global climate change. It not only sets up an energy cooperation platform for the countries along the line but also helps the relevant national economies to follow an environmentally-friendly path.

The BRI is an excellent opportunity to promote multilateralism. More than one hundred countries from all continents have participated in the construction of the project, and they believed it to be a chance to create prosperity and alleviate poverty.

Solheim said many places in the world are still polluted. "We have always been looking for such a treatment scheme to achieve the win-win for industry, environment, and health protection."

He expressed his appreciation for the determination and courage of Chinese leaders to lead the Chinese people to overcome various difficulties. He believes the success of the anti-poverty movement has motivated China to continue to solve climate problems following a development-oriented leadership, detailed data, a well-planned scheme, and practical policies. Under this development model, China is expected to achieve the goal of peak carbon dioxide emissions and carbon neutralization through the combination of ecological civilization and economic development. This is not easy, but it is feasible.

Poverty alleviation and environmental protection are two sides of a coin.

In recent years, a new developmental concept has been widely accepted in China and around the world. It is a concept regarding "ecological civilization" that enables the integrated development of the economy, environment, and livelihood. As renewable energy gradually replaces coal and other fossil fuels, "ecological civilization" is also becoming a reality.

The "Elephant" Station

The Boten–Vientiane railway was put into use on December 3, 2021. Passengers could travel from Kunming (China) to Vientiane (Laos) in just ten hours. The railway was an important docking project of the Chinese BRI and the Laos "from land-bound to land-connected plan." It is also the first international railway built mainly with Chinese investment and with Chinese equipment, built with Chinese equipment, measured by the Chinese standards, and connected directly with China's railway network.

Among the eleven stations along the railway, there is one called the "elephant station"—the Wild Elephant Valley Station. The station is located in Mengyang Township, Jinghong City, Xishuangbanna Prefecture, Yunnan Province. It is named after Wild Elephant Valley, Mengyang Sub-Reserve of the Xishuangbanna National Nature Reserve.

The Wild Elephant Valley Station is a transit station of more than 1.3 square kilometers. The station building is about 2,500 square meters and can house a maximum capacity of four hundred people. The station building is designed based on the theme of "tropical rainforest and natural Wild Elephant Valley." The exterior of the building resembles an Asian elephant with pointed tusks walking in the tropical rainforest. The interior decorations include elements such as "elephant spraying water" and "elephant wandering around," which are highly unique to the regional culture.

It is worth mentioning that the design of Boten-Vientiane railway in China has fully taken into account the Asian elephants' distribution and migration routes. The railway avoids the main activities area of the Asian elephants, and measures such as extending tunnels and replacing roads with bridges were taken to reduce the impact of the railway construction on the ecological environment.

HOMELAND OF DREAMS

4

China and Ecological Civilization

How to tell the Chinese story to the world? How to help the world hear and understand the voice of China? The story of the Short Trunks provides an excellent example.

How to better introduce China to the world? In short, we can summarize the ideas and achievements of China's development in various fields and translate them into foreign languages so that readers in different countries can read and comprehend and that the coverage and influence of China's international communication can be enhanced.

The Keywords to Understand China project was initiated by the China International Communications Group (CICG) and the China Academy of Translation, and it was executed by the Translators Association of China (TAC) and the Center for International Communication Studies. The project established an expert committee on Chinese compilation and multilingual foreign translation composed of experts from relevant Central departments, and it invited foreign experts to participate in the review of the translation. The project is a platform for the international community to access and interpret the development concept, path, domestic and foreign policies, ideological and cultural core discourse of contemporary China in multilingual and multimedia ways. It is a beneficial measure and innovative practice to build a political discourse system integrating China and other countries.

150

At present, by giving concise interpretation on keywords, the project has published books in Chinese, English, French, Russian, Arabic, Spanish, and Japanese. Each book provides text both in Chinese and in the target language so that the readers can understand the content better.

Keywords to Understand China aims to accurately and effectively convey China's development philosophy and domestic and foreign policies, and help export Chinese culture and stories. The project continues to launch *Keywords to Understand China* related multimedia and multi-modal products such as multilingual books, e-books, and short videos every year. These products have been well received among all parties.

Every time the CPC Central Committee holds an important meeting, issues new major policies, and formulates important documents, the Keywords to Understand China project will follow up in time and actively explain the important ideas. In addition, when important changes take place in Chinese society and when representative people, groups, and deeds emerge, the Keywords to Understand China project will also report on them in special columns.

The results of the project are continuously updated on the multilingual website of Keywords to Understand China and modern multimedia platforms. These can serve political parties, dignitaries, think tanks, media, and research institutions in various countries as well as provide an important reference for the work of China's foreign affairs, publicity departments, and embassies and consulates abroad.

On October 9, 2021, at the Erhai Forum in Dali, the Academy of Contemporary China and World Studies released the multilingual version of *Keywords to Understand China: On Ecological Civilization* and a series of multilingual, multimedia, and multi-form products. These products aimed to show the Chinese wisdom, plans, and responsibilities in the field of ecological civilization in the new era, convey China's good will to jointly build ecological civilization, and protect the global environment with the international community.

Keywords to Understand China: On Ecological Civilization includes eighty keywords such as "Xi Jinping's thought on ecological civilization," "harmony between man and nature," "lucid waters and lush mountains are invaluable assets," "the system of institutions for building an ecological civilization," and "keep the sky blue." The book gives brief explanations on each of them to help foreign readers access the Chinese experience, practices, and suggestions on ecological civilization construction. There are four sections in the book: important ideas, key constructions, mechanism and system, and typical cases.

In "Important Ideas" part, the book systematically introduces the background, content, and connotation of twelve ideas such as "Xi Jinping's thought on ecological civilization," "a socialist approach to ecological civilization," and "new concept for development." In "Key Constructions" part, it lists the key environmental protection objectives and work areas proposed by China, such as the "an economic structure facilitating green, low-carbon and circular development," "carbon peak and carbon neutrality," and "biodiversity conservation projects." The chapter of "Mechanism and System" introduces in detail various systems of environmental protection and ecological civilization construction currently adopted in China, such as the "the system of institutions for building an ecological civilization," "the system of property rights of natural resource asset," "the system of protected areas composed mainly of national parks," and "the system of central inspection on environmental protection." The "Typical Cases" shows the outstanding achievements in China's ecological civilization construction over the years and fully illustrates the remarkable results of China's environmental governance, such as the "Anji County: cherishing lucid waters and lush mountains," "Saihanba: ecological restoration," "Kubuqi Model: turning desert into green," "Dulongjiang Township: poverty alleviation along with ecological conservation," and more.

The Academy of Contemporary China and World Studies summarizes the major characteristics of *Keywords to Understand China: On Ecological Civilization* as follows:

First, it explains China's ecological civilization concept of seeking harmonious coexistence between humans and nature. Ideas are the guide to action. Since the 18th National Congress of the CPC, China has written the construction of ecological civilization into the constitution, incorporated it into the overall layout of socialism with Chinese characteristics, and put forward a series of new ideas and new strategies on ecological civilization. *Keywords to Understand China: On Ecological Civilization* focuses on the core concepts of "harmony between man and nature," "lucid waters and lush mountains are invaluable assets," "green development," and "a beautiful China," which clearly expound on China's ecological understanding of respecting, accommodating, and protecting nature and explain China's development abiding by the harmonious coexistence guidelines.

Second, it explains China's policies and actions adhering to green and low-carbon circular development. Actions are the practice of ideas. In the new era, China follows the new development concepts of innovation, coordination, environmentally friendly, openness, and sharing, adopts a holistic approach to conserving the mountains, rivers, forests, farmlands, lakes, and grasslands, takes the road of green, low-carbon and circular development, and is committed to building a beautiful China with "mountains and waters in sight, and nostalgia in mind." *Keywords to Understand China: On Ecological Civilization* focuses on policy actions such as "territorial space development and protection," "rural revitalization strategy," "carbon peak and carbon neutrality," and "biodiversity conservation projects." It systematically introduces China's ongoing ecological civilization system, the overall green transformation of economic and social development, as well as the ongoing practice of ecological restoration and environmental governance. It provides a useful reference for promoting global green development.

Third, the book demonstrates China's global initiative to build a community of humans and nature. Building a green homeland is the common dream of mankind. Contemporary China firmly practices multilateralism and strives to be an important participant, contributor, and leader in the construction of global ecological civilization. *Keywords to Understand China: On Ecological Civilization* focuses on programs and initiatives such as "global environmental governance," "addressing climate change," "energy revolution," and "conservation of marine eco-environment" to fully describe China's sincerity in building a clean, beautiful, and harmonious world with all countries and realize global sustainable development and all-round human development.

In addition to the *Keywords to Understand China: On Ecological civilization*, the Keywords to Understand China project has also focused on many important areas related to the national economy and people's livelihood, such as the Chinese Dream, national defense and military development, targeted poverty alleviation, foreign affairs in the new era, comprehensively deepening reform, etc. These projects actively share China's wisdom with the world, promote the construction of a community of human and natural lives, and help the world understand China better.

Afterword

A letter from the Short Trunks to the world

Dear human friends,

How are you?

It's autumn now, and Mom said it's time to go home. So, we chose the very lucky day of the closing of the Olympic Games on August 8, 2021, to return to the south. We crossed the Yuanjiang River and embarked on the way home.

It was in the bright spring of March 2020. Our family started the journey all the way to the north because we wanted to see this huge, amazing world.

We have always heard that the place where we were was called Yunnan, and we always thought that only the rainforest where we lived was Yunnan. However, when we came out, we realized that Yunnan was much larger than we thought. We walked for five hundred days and for more than a thousand kilometers, but we were still in Yunnan.

It was such a big and interesting place to see! We learned so much on our trip. Outside our habitat, there are forests, grasslands, and streams that we know well, but there are also high-rise buildings, villages, and "mechanical animals" running on the road all day long.

At first, we were worried that the trip would be difficult after we left our forest. But when we started it, we found beautiful flowers and towering trees all the way. Sometimes when we were hungry, we went into the cornfield to eat. Not only did the owners not curse us or drive us away, but they also kept sending us more of our favorite crops.

The villages we came across were so beautiful. We went in several households and tried the tap water. It was as clear and sweet as the water in the forests. We love the outside world very much, but we have small regrets too. For example, we did not have the chance to try the famous rice noodles. You gave us so much corn and bananas, but we also wanted to try something new. Who knows? Maybe we would really like it! It's a shame that we did not make it to COP15 at the International Exhibit Center in Yunnan or visit the "hundred-mile Dianchi Lake." We had planned to admire the "sleeping beauty" from afar, but then we thought it's better not to disturb her sleep, so we changed our mind.

Of course, what I remember the most is you, our human friends. You were so kind to give us food, make way for us, and guide us with the high-tech machines that fly above us here and there. It was very easy to follow them.

But you did "bad" things too. You posted everything about us online. The way we sleep, our little family arguments, our childish games and fights, and the little one's clumsiness when learning to walk ... not only everyone in China but also many around the world have seen our "private" pictures. It's so embarrassing!

Actually, we updated our "social media" along our trip too. The Yunnan snub-nosed monkeys, the green peafowls, and the black-necked cranes who saw our "posts" were all very jealous and said they would love to see it as well. Our African relatives also followed us on our platform and gave us thumbs up.

Anyway, we would like to thank you for everything you have done for us. We had a great time both on our way north and on our way back. We did a lot of sightseeing and ate a lot of good food. More importantly, we knew better about you. Your kindness made us realize that we could live in harmony. The earth is our home. Let's take care of her as our mother!

We didn't prepare for our trip very well before we left. Sorry about all the trouble we caused you this time! We will be more careful next time.

Thank you again! We hope our homeland will get better and better!

A group of happy Asian elephants on their way home
August 8, 2021

Index

ABOUT THE AUTHORS

The writing group of this book is mainly composed of journalists and writers who have long paid attention to China's ecological environment. During the northbound migration process of the Asian elephants in Yunnan, they either "chased" the elephants and collected authentic materials on the frontline or wrote the press to support these "model elephants" in the rear. They presented to the readers a large number of news reports directly from the Yunnan rainforest with fresh soil and dew. Based on rich and real material, they compiled and published a series of books including *Travel Notes of Wild Elephants in Yunnan*, *Cute Elephants Love Yunnan*, and *Travel Notes of the Short Trunks*.